4-5-73

LECTURES IN ECONOMICS, 2

INTRODUCTORY ECONOMETRICS

Kenneth F. Wallis

The London School of Economics and Political Science

ALDINE PUBLISHING COMPANY
Chicago

About the Author

After completing studies at the University of Manchester, Kenneth Wallis received his Ph.D. from Stanford University in 1966. He is presently a Reader in Statistics (with Special Reference to Econometrics) at the London School of Economics.

LECTURES IN ECONOMICS

1 *Macroeconomics and Monetary Theory* by Harry G. Johnson
2 *Introductory Econometrics* by Kenneth F. Wallis

First published in Great Britain, 1972

First U.S. edition published 1972 by
Aldine Publishing Company
529 South Wabash Avenue
Chicago, Illinois 60605

ISBN 0-202-06055-1 cloth
ISBN 0-202-06056- x paper
Library of Congress Catalog Number 72-87566

Printed in the United States of America

CONTENTS

PREFACE

This book is based on a course of lectures given at the London School of Economics in recent years to students on the M.Sc. course in Economics, as part of the teaching under the general heading of Methods of Economic Investigation. In the session 1970-71 these lectures were tape-recorded and transcribed by Hamish Gray, and the resulting notes, with errors corrected and major blemishes removed, were made available to the students on the course. Further editing has subsequently taken place, and some new paragraphs have been inserted, but the material essentially remains as lecture notes. These are now offered not only for the continuing use of students at the School, but also to any student or practising economist who wishes to obtain an introduction to the methods of econometrics.

The aim of this book is to encourage an appreciation of the problems of empirical measurement of economic relationships, and an assessment of the techniques by which those problems may be solved. This will further help the student of economics to understand the ever-increasing literature reporting the results of applied econometric studies, and to ask the right questions when beginning his own empirical research. However, this book will not turn the reader into a fledgling econometric theoretician, for it is not our purpose to present an account of the statistical theory underlying econometric estimation methods – in any case an adequate selection of such accounts already exists in textbook form. In accordance with these objectives, the course begins with a discussion of economic models and the presentation of economic theories in a form suitable for estimation and testing. A simple national income determination system is used as an example, initially in static form but subsequently extended to illustrate the discussion of dynamic behaviour. The identification problem is presented in terms of familiar demand-and-supply models, and estimation methods are described in the last (and longest) chapter.

The prerequisites for this book are courses in matrix algebra and elementary statistics. At LSE such courses are included in a one-month crash programme for those admitted to the one-year M.Sc. course without an adequate background in the quantitative area, (see for example G. Mills, *Introduction to Linear Algebra for Social Scientists,* (Allen and Unwin), and J. J. Thomas, *An Introduction to Statistical Theory for Economists,* (Weidenfeld and Nicholson)). With respect to the mathematical and statistical material, familiarity with basic ideas and techniques is more important than coverage of advanced topics. Thus, the matrix representation of a system of simultaneous linear equations is used from Chapter 2 onwards, but such matters as eigenvalues and eigenvectors never appear. Likewise, the expectation operator appears at an early stage. While an elementary statistics course would undoubtedly include the theory of the simple linear regression model, this is sketched at the start of Chapter 5, on estimation, in order to achieve a complete and unified treatment. Again, however, this chapter aims to provide an understanding of some estimation methods and their applicability, and rigorous proofs of the statistical properties of such estimators are not presented. It is difficult to specify a particular prerequisite in economics, but some knowledge of economics is obviously assumed from the beginning, for this is a course given to graduate students. Such students have many and diverse special fields of interest, so the details of specific applications of the general ideas discussed here to a particular area of economics are often left to the reader.

The teaching for Methods of Economic Investigation also includes lectures on "Case Studies" or applications, hence no applied work is discussed in detail in the present volume. Preliminary material for the applied section is contained in the last three chapters of J. S.Cramer, *Empirical Econometrics* (North-Holland) and, at a somewhat more elementary level, Part IV of A. A. Walters, *An Introduction to Econometrics* (Macmillan); the actual topics covered vary from year to year, as does the list of readings. Lectures in both parts of the course are supplemented by classes, and a selection of the problems used in such classes is printed at the end of each chapter. These, together with the five review problems, include questions from past examination papers. Outline solutions to even-numbered problems are given at the end of the book.

Ever since this course was first given at LSE, the recommended textbook has been C. F. Christ, *Econometric Models and Methods* (Wiley), and anyone familiar with that book will recognise the enormous intellectual debt this book owes to it. This is particularly true of Part Two of *Econometric Models and Methods*, on theoretical models, which was something of an innovation when the book first appeared, for the vast majority of econometrics textbooks are concerned solely with estimation theory. Needless to say, *Econometric Models and Methods* provides further reading on virtually every topic discussed in these lectures; in addition, review material on basic statistical theory and matrix algebra is contained in Chapter IV and Appendix A respectively. I am grateful to Professor Christ for making his material freely available to me for the purpose of certain sections of the present volume.

My colleagues David F. Hendry, David J. Reid and J. J. Thomas, who assisted by taking classes in 1970-71, have made helpful comments on this material, for which I am grateful while retaining sole responsibility for errors. I am indebted to Carol Martin for her expert typing of the original notes, and for patiently coping with the subsequent revisions.

Chapter 1

INTRODUCTION

Rather than begin with an attempted definition of econometrics we may briefly but usefully distinguish it from its near relations – mathematical economics and economic statistics. The former is concerned with economic theory and its formulation using mathematical techniques, notation and language. The main interest lies in the mathematical properties of economic systems and no concession is typically made to measurability or empirical verification of propositions. The economic statistician on the other hand is concerned with collecting and presenting economic data. While the analysis undertaken on the resulting statistics is often quite sophisticated, involving very elaborate methods for constructing index numbers or seasonally adjusting economic time series, the economic statistician seldom goes much further than analysing series or variables one at a time. Indeed when he does so I would say he is beginning to get into econometrics.

What distinguishes econometrics from these two fields is its foundation in measurement and empirical testing of hypotheses. We use the output of the economic statistician to quantify relationships between variables which explain their observed behaviour and which may also be used for prediction. We have a multivariate approach to contrast with his univariate approach. We draw on mathematical economics for the formulation and specification of hypotheses. While the theorist's reasoning may lead to statements about the relationships between economic variables expressed algebraically, statements about the response of certain variables to particular changes in the system are usually of a qualitative nature, describing the direction or sign of the response for example, and they are seldom quantitative – the magnitude of the response is not specified. Any numerical illustrations use assumed values of coefficients. We attempt to fill this gap by obtaining such values from observations on the economic variables, and by measuring responses, thus estimation is basic to econometric procedure. Though we shall not discuss estimation methods for a while most of the early part of the book is aimed at facilitating the measurement and empirical testing of relationships among variables, and the use of these relationships for analysis and prediction.

Chapter 2

BASIC CONCEPTS, TERMINOLOGY, AND NOTATION

2.1 *Economic structure and the model*

We introduce the basic concepts by means of a simple static, exact example. This is a two-equation, Keynesian-type national income determination system, which we shall subsequently extend in various ways. The first equation is an accounting identity or income definition in which income comprises consumption and autonomous expenditure ($y = c + i$). This does not relate the variables it contains in the only possible way, for we also have a consumption function expressing consumption as a function of income ($c = f(y)$) and the theory suggests that f is an increasing function.

In order that we may solve the system we need to assume a specific functional form and for convenience we shall assume that the function is linear ($c = \alpha + \beta y$). It will then possess properties specified for the Keynesian consumption function if the constant term α is positive ($\alpha > 0$) and the slope coefficient is between zero and one ($0 < \beta < 1$). The assumption embodied in this specialisation of a general to a linear function may seen outrageous. However, we can regard the linear function as an approximation to the general function in the particular range of its variation where we happen to be working, that is, over a small range of variation of y (cf. linear approximation of curve in elementary mathematics).

We shall refer to the equations

$$y = c + i$$
$$c = \alpha + \beta y$$

as *structural equations.* The first equation is an *identity* and the second is a *behavioural equation* i.e. a relationship which describes economic agents' behaviour rather than a relationship which is true in a balance sheet sense. The behavioural relationship may be regarded as asymmetrical in that 'causality' works from right to left.

The *economic structure* is the whole set of features which remains constant over a particular period of investigation (*observation period*). This covers the form of the equations and the numerical values of the constants α and β (which are called *structural parameters* or structural coefficients). The set of structures obtained as α and β take different values is referred to as the *model*. The model therefore contains all the (a priori) information available before any empirical testing or measurement has taken place, that is, the form of the equations, leaving the values of the parameters unspecified. For theoretical reasons we might want to put further restrictions on coefficients (e.g. $0 < \beta < 1$) without specifying a particular value for them. The theory then tells us something about the responsiveness of the system in a qualitative way (e.g. directions of change) but it can rarely tell us anything numerically specific. Information about such features as the magnitude of change or the frequency of oscillations in dynamic systems (discussed later) can arise only from estimation.

It is useful to distinguish variables which the system is designed to explain – *endogenous variables* – from those which are determined outside the system – *exogenous variables*. We regard a model as incompletely defined by the equation-system, or set of structures; we also require a statement as to which variables are endogenous and which exogenous. In our simple illustrative system c and y are endogenous variables and are explained in terms of the variable i, which is exogenous and does not depend on c or y (hence its usual description as autonomous expenditure).

Suppose that we now make consumption a function of disposable income, writing

$$c = \alpha + \beta(y - t)$$

where t = taxes. Then whether t is regarded as an exogenous variable or a structural parameter depends on whether or not it varies during the observation period. If t does not change it becomes a structural parameter.

For the system to be consistent (i.e. to have a determinate solution giving unique values of the endogenous variables in terms of structural parameters and exogenous variables) we require that the number of equations in the model be the same as the number of endogenous variables.

2.2 *Structural form, reduced form, and prediction*

To see how this solution is obtained, we begin with our two equation model in its structural form:

$$y = c + i$$
$$c = \alpha + \beta(y - t)$$

endogenous variables: y, c

exogenous variables: i, t.

Substituting for c in the first equation gives

$$y = \alpha + \beta(y - t) + i$$

which yields, upon rearrangement,

$$y = \frac{1}{1-\beta}(\alpha - \beta t + i).$$

Then

$$c = \frac{1}{1-\beta}(\alpha - \beta t + \beta i).$$

The last pair of equations is known as the *reduced form,* which tells us how the endogenous variables vary with or are determined by the exogenous variables alone. Reduced form equations do not directly describe economic agents' behaviour, but tell us the results of that behaviour on the endogenous variables, taken one at a time.

Often it is useful to write out the reduced form in a more general way as follows:

$$y = \pi_1 + \pi_2 t + \pi_3 i$$
$$c = \pi_4 + \pi_5 t + \pi_6 i$$

where the π's (π_i, $i = 1,...,6$) are *reduced form parameters* or coefficients and are functions (generally non-linear) of the structural parameters, ($\pi_1 = \frac{\alpha}{1-\beta}$, $\pi_2 = \frac{-\beta}{1-\beta}$, etc.).

Note that the a priori information or the form of the model imposes restrictions on the reduced form parameters: there are six π_i but the structural form contains only two structural parameters α and β, (assuming i and t vary over the observation period) and we require that

$$\pi_2 = \pi_5 = -\pi_6, \qquad \pi_1 = \pi_4, \qquad \pi_3 - \pi_6 = 1.$$

If we are interested in predicting what values of y and c will result from given values of i and t then we only need to know the reduced form coefficients. If the government wished to achieve a particular target level of the endogenous variable y by assigning values of the exogenous variables i and t (using i and t as policy instruments) then all it would need to know would be the first reduced form equation with particular numerical values specified or estimated for π_1, π_2, and π_3. However, this really requires the assumption that the economic structure does not change between the observation and prediction periods. The information in the reduced form is not sufficient if the structure is going to change, for then we shall need to go back to structural parameters and hope to be able to reformulate the model to take account of the change. Having defined the structure as incorporating specific values of the structural parameters, a simple example of a structural change is a change in one of these values, say an increase in β from 0.8 to 0.9. Then we could deduce a new reduced form from knowledge of the old structural parameters plus our knowledge of the way in whicn these had changed, and use this to predict in the changed structure. Thus an estimated reduced form equation is an adequate prediction device only as long as one is willing to assume an absence of structural change.

2.3 *Segmentability*

Now let us modify our example by distinguishing between public and private investment, making public investment (g) exogenous and relating private investment (i) to the familiar marginal efficiency of investment approach. Thus i becomes endogenous and is some general function of the interest rate (r) with, a priori, a negative first derivative. Again we represent it as a linear function over the range of variation we are interested in:

$$i = \gamma + \delta r$$

(continuing the convention of denoting structural parameters by greek letters).

So we now have a three equation model

$$\begin{aligned} y &= c + i + g \\ c &= \alpha + \beta(y - t) \\ i &= \gamma + \delta r \end{aligned} \qquad \begin{aligned} &\text{endogenous:} \quad y, c, i \\ &\text{exogenous:} \quad g, t, r \end{aligned}$$

As before we have the same number of equations as endogenous variables so we can solve the system to get the reduced form. On doing so, however, we see that the reduced form equation for private investment (i) is precisely the same as the third structural equation. Whereas in the previous section we described the difference between structural equations and reduced form equations, now we see that there are occasions on which the two are algebraically indistinguishable. This also provides an example of a model which is *segmentable.*

In general a segmentable model is one which can be split into segments each of which determines a set of the endogenous variables by themselves within that segment, and without reference to other endogenous variables in later segments. 'Later' may be interpreted either in a causal chain sense or in terms of a sequential solution. In our model the third equation represents a segment. We first determine investment by the interest rate and then may regard investment as given in a certain sense when we come to the remaining two equations to determine y and c; there is no feedback between income or consumption and investment.

Our illustration of a segmentable model has the property that one segment has identical structural and reduced form equations, but this does not necessarily generalise. Here it is the case because the segment contains only one equation, which is logically prior to all others. If it were the case that our model determined the interest rate in terms of further exogenous variables and investment (!), but not c or y, then we would have a two equation segment and there would not be any correspondence between behavioural (structural) equations and reduced form equations even in the segment.

2.4 *Time series and cross-section models; aggregation*

We have said that the structure remains constant during an observation period and the connotation has been that of a *time series model.* To make that clear we could attach a time subscript (t) to each variable and write out (say) the consumption function as $c_t = \alpha + \beta y_t$ and define the range of t as $t = 1,...,T$. Now the observation period is clearly defined in terms of these T observations (separated by weeks, months, quarters, years etc.). The data are in the form of time series, and if these are aggregate data we have a time series model of the aggregate consumption function assuming α and β remain constant during the T observations. Prediction or forecasting is then concerned with estimating the values of the variables at time $t = T + 1, T + 2,....$

In a *cross-section model* we may have the same sort of consumption fuction but now the data relate to different units of observation at a given point in time. Let us suppose that we have a cross-section sample of N households from some family expenditure survey. Then we may write

$$c_i = \alpha + \beta y_i \qquad\qquad i = 1,...,N$$

and assume that the behaviour of all N households may be described by this equation, with α and β constant. Although we might continue to use the term *observation period* for the sample of observations, $i = 1,...,N$, the term here has no time connotation at all. The concept of prediction however still has a very obvious counterpart, for in the cross-section case prediction refers to an estimate of the behaviour of unobserved elements in the population (households who have not been sampled).

Clearly, a model or an equation or simply data can be in both time series and cross-section form. Suppose we have a cross-section of N individual households over a time series of T periods (say, years). The consumption and income of the ith household at time t may be written c_{it}, y_{it}, $i=1,...,N$, $t=1,...,T$ and these observations are known as *panel data.* (It is assumed that the same N households are observed for T years, rather than that a fresh sample of N is drawn each year.)

An interesting point about this type of study is that whereas one is often ready to put a priori restrictions on a system in aggregate models (e.g. $0 < \beta < 1$), in a large proportion of cases they are based upon arguments about the behaviour of the individual micro unit. It may be possible to rationalise the behaviour of an individual consumer and come up with restrictions on the parameters of an aggregate function, but there is a sequence of steps implied that is too often overlooked. In proceeding from a micro-model to an aggregate relation, we distinguish between *aggregation of variables* and *aggregation of equations.* It is fairly easy to define the aggregate variables C_t, Y_t as

$$C_t = \sum_{i=1}^{N} c_{it}, \qquad Y_t = \sum_{i=1}^{N} y_{it}, \qquad t = 1,...,T.$$

But suppose each household has its own consumption function

$$c_{it} = \alpha_i + \beta_i y_{it} \qquad t = 1,...,T$$

– a time series equation for the ith household, with α_i and β_i constant over the T observations but possibly different between households. Under what conditions will we get an aggregate consumption function relating aggregate variables in the same way (linearly, with constant coefficients)? Upon aggregating the equations

$$\begin{aligned} c_{1t} &= \alpha_1 + \beta_1 y_{1t} \\ c_{2t} &= \alpha_2 + \beta_2 y_{2t} \\ &\cdot \\ &\cdot \\ &\cdot \\ c_{Nt} &= \alpha_N + \beta_N y_{Nt} \end{aligned}$$

the left hand side gives C_t, and the first term on the right presents no problem for we simply define the aggregate intercept term α as the sum of the α_i's:

$$\alpha = \sum_{i=1}^{N} \alpha_i .$$

But the second term will give βY_t (with constant β) *only if* all the β_i are the same, i.e. $\beta_1 = \beta_2 = ... = \beta_N = \beta$, say, whereupon

$$\Sigma\, \beta_i y_{it} = \beta \Sigma y_{it} = \beta Y_t .$$

Thus if all the micro-level mpc's (β_i) are constant and equal, we have

$$C_t = \alpha + \beta Y_t, \qquad t = 1,...,T.$$

Sometimes one can go further in deriving a linear aggregate relationship from micro functions. The following example illustrates a point about the usefulness of outside information. Suppose we know the income distribution independently. We then know the (constant) share in aggregate income of each individual household, and can replace the individual income variables by the ith household's share of total income at each point in time i.e. $y_{it} = \lambda_i Y_t$, $t = 1,\ldots,T$. where the constants $\lambda_1, \lambda_2, \ldots, \lambda_N$, with $\Sigma\lambda_i = 1$, are given to us from outside. We then end up with a reasonable aggregate equation with a readily interpretable parameter. Our micro system now is

$$
\begin{aligned}
c_{1t} &= \alpha_1 + \beta_1 \lambda_1 Y_t \\
c_{2t} &= \alpha_2 + \beta_2 \lambda_2 Y_t \\
&\cdot \\
&\cdot \\
&\cdot \\
c_{Nt} &= \alpha_N + \beta_N \lambda_N Y_t
\end{aligned}
$$

and aggregating yields the linear relation with constant parameters

$$C_t = \alpha + \beta Y_t$$

where α is as above and β is defined by

$$\beta = \sum_{i=1}^{N} \lambda_i \beta_i$$

– a weighted average of mpc's with weights depending on the (given) income share of each micro unit.

Note that it would not be sufficient to take our earlier micro system and write for each time period

$$\sum_{i=1}^{N} \beta_i y_{it} = \beta^* Y_t,$$

defining the "aggregate mpc" as the weighted average

$$\beta^* = \sum_{i=1}^{N} \frac{y_{it}}{Y_t} \beta_i = \frac{\Sigma y_{it} \beta_i}{\Sigma y_{it}},$$

for the weights vary over time, and the term $\beta^* Y_t$ is not linear in aggregate income, with constant coefficient.

2.5 *General notation for linear models*

To avoid constructing an increasingly complicated national income model as we proceed to illustrate econometric methods it is useful to present a general notation for linear models. There are some relatively standard conventions which we now describe.

Endogenous variables are denoted by y's and exogenous variables by z's. The number of endogenous variables (and structural equations) is denoted by G, and there are K exogenous variables, thus $y_1, y_2, \ldots, y_G$ are the endogenous variables and $z_1, z_2, \ldots, z_K$ the exogenous variables of the system. Parameters for endogenous variables are denoted by β's. They have two subscripts, the first – or row subscript – for the equation in question and the second – or column subscript – for the particular variable to which the coefficient is attached. Parameters of exogenous variables are denoted by γ's (again the first subscript for the equation and the second for the exogenous variable in question).

We can write out the standard form for linear models in several ways. Collecting all terms on the left hand side, we may write the G structural equations as follows:

$$\begin{array}{l}
\beta_{11}y_1 + \beta_{12}y_2 + \ldots + \beta_{1G}y_G + \gamma_{11}z_1 + \gamma_{12}z_2 + \ldots + \gamma_{1K}z_K = 0 \\
\beta_{21}y_1 + \beta_{22}y_2 + \ldots + \beta_{2G}y_G + \gamma_{21}z_1 + \gamma_{22}z_2 + \ldots + \gamma_{2K}z_K = 0 \\
\cdot \qquad\qquad\qquad\qquad\qquad\qquad\qquad\qquad\qquad\qquad \cdot \\
\cdot \qquad\qquad\qquad\qquad\qquad\qquad\qquad\qquad\qquad\qquad \cdot \\
\cdot \qquad\qquad\qquad\qquad\qquad\qquad\qquad\qquad\qquad\qquad \cdot \\
\beta_{G1}y_1 + \beta_{G2}y_2 + \ldots + \beta_{GG}y_G + \gamma_{G1}z_1 + \gamma_{G2}z_2 + \ldots + \gamma_{GK}z_K = 0
\end{array}$$

Restrictions on the parameters would be determined by what the equations represented. For example, if the first equation was a consumption function in a conventional national income model, and in this equation consumption (denoted by y_1 say) and income (y_2) were the only endogenous variables and there were no exogenous variables appearing, we would represent this by restricting $\beta_{13}, \beta_{14}, \ldots, \beta_{1G}$ and γ_{1k}, $k=1,\ldots,K$ to be zero. This illustrates one way in which this general framework may represent a particular behavioural equation – by imposing zero restrictions on appropriate parameters. If an equation were an identity then we would restrict the parameters of the variables appearing to (say) equal 1's or −1's. A constant term (intercept) in any equation is easily handled by assigning the value 1 to a particular exogenous variable e.g. $z_K = 1$, then its coefficients in different equations (γ_{gK}, $g = 1,\ldots,G$) are intercept terms. A problem arises because each equation remains true when we multiply it through by a constant, so there is some indeterminacy in the parameter values. We can remove that indeterminacy by imposing a *normalisation* rule so that the parameters have unique numerical values. A conventional way is to restrict the coefficient of the ith endogenous variable in the ith equation to equal one ($\beta_{ii} = 1$). Thus, if that equation is a behavioural equation we are regarding it as the structural equation primarily concerned with the ith endogenous variable (y_i).

If our objective was to construct a notation for discussing general ideas without constructing a more and more complicated illustrative model as we go along, we have gained very little so far. There are two ways of reducing the mess to manageable proportions, first by the use of standard summation notation and second by matrix algebra.

The gth equation may first be written

$$\sum_{i=1}^{G} \beta_{gi} y_i + \sum_{k=1}^{K} \gamma_{gk} z_k = 0$$

and $g = 1,\ldots,G$. Again, the general model can be written in matrix form:

$$\begin{bmatrix} \beta_{11} & \beta_{12} & \cdots & \beta_{1G} \\ \beta_{21} & \beta_{22} & \cdots & \beta_{2G} \\ \cdot & & & \cdot \\ \cdot & & & \cdot \\ \cdot & & & \cdot \\ \beta_{G1} & \beta_{G2} & \cdots & \beta_{GG} \end{bmatrix} \begin{bmatrix} y_1 \\ y_2 \\ \cdot \\ \cdot \\ \cdot \\ y_G \end{bmatrix} + \begin{bmatrix} \gamma_{11} & \gamma_{12} & \cdots & \gamma_{1K} \\ \gamma_{21} & \gamma_{22} & \cdots & \gamma_{2K} \\ \cdot & & & \cdot \\ \cdot & & & \cdot \\ \cdot & & & \cdot \\ \gamma_{G1} & \gamma_{G2} & \cdots & \gamma_{GK} \end{bmatrix} \begin{bmatrix} z_1 \\ z_2 \\ \cdot \\ \cdot \\ \cdot \\ z_K \end{bmatrix} = \begin{bmatrix} 0 \\ 0 \\ \cdot \\ \cdot \\ \cdot \\ 0 \end{bmatrix}$$

Defining **B** and **Γ** as the above matrices of structural parameters, and **y** and **z** as the above column vectors of endogenous and exogenous variables respectively, we have

$$\mathbf{By} + \mathbf{\Gamma z} = \mathbf{0}.$$

Since the number of equations is equal to the number of endogenous variables **B** is always square $(G \times G)$ but nothing is said about whether Γ $(G \times K)$ is square or not. There may be more or fewer exogenous variables than equations (endogenous variables).

We can introduce a few of the points from our previous example in terms of this general notation. The three-equation model, writing the investment equation (segmentable) first, and re-arranging terms, is

$$\begin{array}{lllll} i & -\delta r & & -\gamma & = 0 \\ c - \beta y & & +\beta t & -\alpha & = 0 \\ -i - c + y & -g & & & = 0 \end{array}$$

The variables are i,c,y endogenous, and r,g,t exogenous. This alphabetical notation restricts us to 26 variables, so let us relabel them

$$\begin{array}{ll} i = y_1 & r = z_1 \\ c = y_2 & g = z_2 \\ y = y_3 & t = z_3 \end{array}$$

and introduce a constant term by defining $z_4 = 1$. We have aligned variables in columns so that the system can be almost immediately translated into matrix form, as follows

$$\begin{bmatrix} 1 & 0 & 0 \\ 0 & 1 & -\beta \\ -1 & -1 & 1 \end{bmatrix} \begin{bmatrix} y_1 \\ y_2 \\ y_3 \end{bmatrix} + \begin{bmatrix} -\delta & 0 & 0 & -\gamma \\ 0 & 0 & \beta & -\alpha \\ 0 & -1 & 0 & 0 \end{bmatrix} \begin{bmatrix} z_1 \\ z_2 \\ z_3 \\ z_4 \end{bmatrix} = \begin{bmatrix} 0 \\ 0 \\ 0 \end{bmatrix}$$

We see that the square matrix **B** has 1's along its main diagonal – the normalisation rule. The intercept (constant) terms are given by the last column of Γ, since we have defined $z_4 = 1$. The identity can be picked out, as the *values* of its structural parameters are specified a priori – to be 1 or -1.

We said that the most common way of incorporating a priori information was to impose zero restrictions on appropriate coefficients (i.e. to exclude variables from certain equations) and this can be illustrated for the investment equation. To say that investment depends on the rate of interest is to imply that it does not depend upon other variables in the model (c,g,t,y) and the four zeros in the first row of the coefficient matrices make this quite clear. Our specification enters in a further way since, in terms of the general notation, we have $\beta_{23} + \gamma_{23} = 0$. This is an example of a homogeneous linear restriction. Here it arises because we have said that, if we define y as aggregate income and t as personal taxes, consumption depends upon disposable income $(y-t)$. Thus, in the equation $c = \alpha + \beta(y-t)$, y and t appear with the same coefficient but with opposite sign. (In the new notation, $y_2 + \beta_{23}y_3 + \gamma_{23}z_3 + \gamma_{24}z_4 = 0$ corresponds to $c - \beta y + \beta t - \alpha = 0$, hence $\beta_{23} + \gamma_{23} = 0$.) Thus the purpose of this restriction is to make it clear that consumption depends upon disposable income. While zero restrictions are probably the most common way of getting theoretical information into the model, they can be seen as special cases of the more general homogeneous linear restriction, for such a special case is precisely what we have when we write $\beta_{12} = 0$.

Finally, the statements we made about segmentability have an interpretation here as well. The segmentability of the model arising from the 'prior' determination of investment is indicated in the present formulation by the block of zeros in the top right hand corner of the **B** matrix. There is therefore no feedback from the endogenous variables determined in the lower segment to the endogenous variable in the upper segment. Segmentability is in general recognisable by a block or blocks of zeros above the main diagonal (assuming the equations are appropriately ordered according to the causal ordering or the sequence of solution – here we can solve for investment first without reference to c or y, so that equation is written first) (cf. decomposability in, for example, R. G. D. Allen's *Mathematical Economics*). If we have larger models with several segments there will be more blocks of zeros above the main diagonal. A four-equation model, for example, which contained two segments could have a **B** matrix obeying one of the following schemes

$$\left[\begin{array}{c|ccc}1&0&0&0\\ \hline *&1&*&*\\ *&*&1&*\\ *&*&*&1\end{array}\right] \quad \left[\begin{array}{cc|cc}1&*&0&0\\ *&1&0&0\\ \hline *&*&1&*\\ *&*&*&1\end{array}\right] \quad \left[\begin{array}{ccc|c}1&*&*&0\\ *&1&*&0\\ *&*&1&0\\ \hline *&*&*&1\end{array}\right]$$

B

representing segments of one and three, or two and two, or three and one equations respectively (asterisks denoting as yet unspecified coefficients). In each case the first block of endogenous variables are determined without reference to endogenous variables appearing in the second block, which are subsequently determined in terms of the solution for the first block. In the second and third examples above, the first equation alone is not segmentable because there is a feedback from y_2 to y_1. The limiting case is that of a triangular **B** matrix with zeros everwhere above the main diagonal, when each equation would be a segment, which provides one of the requirements of a recursive system (to be discussed in Section 5.8).

[The monetary theorist's notion of *dichotomy* might be represented in this framework by a **B** matrix in which the bottom left hand block was also full of zeros – i.e. the model breaks up into two sub-models. It would be difficult to write such a model in this framework, however, for typically the model would not be linear – variables determined in one block (nominal) are functions of, inter alia, variables determined in the other block (real)].

The general *reduced form* of G equations, each determining an endogenous variable in terms of the K exogenous variables, can be written as

$$y_i = \sum_{k=1}^{K} \pi_{ik} z_k, \qquad i=1,\dots,G.$$

or as

$$\begin{bmatrix} y_1 \\ y_2 \\ \cdot \\ \cdot \\ \cdot \\ y_G \end{bmatrix} = \begin{bmatrix} \pi_{11} & \pi_{12} & \dots & \pi_{1K} \\ \pi_{21} & \pi_{22} & & \pi_{2K} \\ \cdot & \cdot & & \cdot \\ \cdot & \cdot & & \cdot \\ \cdot & \cdot & & \cdot \\ \pi_{G1} & \pi_{G2} & & \pi_{GK} \end{bmatrix} \begin{bmatrix} z_1 \\ z_2 \\ \cdot \\ \cdot \\ \cdot \\ z_K \end{bmatrix}$$

or as

$$\mathbf{y} = \mathbf{\Pi} \mathbf{z}$$

where Π is the $G \times K$ matrix of reduced form coefficients. These can be obtained from the structural parameters by solving the structural form as follows:

$$\mathbf{B}\,\mathbf{y} = -\,\mathbf{\Gamma}\,\mathbf{z}$$

therefore $\quad \mathbf{B}^{-1}\mathbf{B}\,\mathbf{y} = -\,\mathbf{B}^{-1}\,\mathbf{\Gamma}\,\mathbf{z}$

i.e. $\quad \mathbf{y} = -\,\mathbf{B}^{-1}\,\mathbf{\Gamma}\,\mathbf{z}$ and hence $\mathbf{\Pi} = -\,\mathbf{B}^{-1}\,\mathbf{\Gamma}$.

Implicit in this derivation is the assumption that the inverse of the $G \times G$ matrix **B** exists. Thus it is being assumed that the determinant of

B is non-zero (that **B** is non-singular), or equivalently that no structural equation is a linear combination of other structural equations.

When we think about some of the large macroeconometric models currently under construction it may appear that solving for the reduced form is very difficult, for inverting a large **B** matrix is a non-trivial task. What makes life a little easier is the benevolence of the theoretician who is cheerfully scattering zeros across the **B** matrix. It might be worth checking as an exercise that the Π matrix of the three equation model discussed previously turns out to be

$$\begin{bmatrix} \delta & 0 & 0 & \gamma \\ \dfrac{\beta\delta}{1-\beta} & \dfrac{\beta}{1-\beta} & \dfrac{-\beta}{1-\beta} & \dfrac{\alpha+\beta\gamma}{1-\beta} \\ \dfrac{\delta}{1-\beta} & \dfrac{1}{1-\beta} & \dfrac{-\beta}{1-\beta} & \dfrac{\alpha+\gamma}{1-\beta} \end{bmatrix}$$

2.6 *Linearity of variables and parameters*

The structural equations we have been discussing are linear both in the parameters (β's and γ's) and in the variables (y's and z's). It is useful to distinguish these two senses, both of which are usually implied when we speak of 'linear models'. In practice the first requirement is the more important, particularly for estimation, and departures from the second can often be easily handled. An example of an equation that is linear in parameters but not in variables can be obtained by generalising the consumption function from a linear to a quadratic function of disposable income:

$$c = \alpha + \beta_1 (y-t) + \beta_2 (y-t)^2 .$$

Linearity in parameters (α, β_1 and β_2) implies that they enter in linear combination with the variables: they are not product or ratio functions of each other – they do not appear to any power. (As illustrated above, reduced form coefficients often provide examples of non-linear functions of structural parameters). The non-linearity of the variables occurs of course because we now have a power of the disposable income variable. This we can sidestep simply by defining $(y-t)^2$ as a new variable. Another common practice is the use of logarithms to transform multiplicative functions into forms linear in parameters. Consider the Cobb-Douglas production function:

$$X = \gamma L^{\alpha} K^{\beta}.$$

All one has to do to make it linear in variables and parameters – it is neither as it stands – is to take logarithms and define new variables:

$$\log X = \log \gamma + \alpha \log L + \beta \log K.$$

Similarly, if constant returns to scale are imposed we require $\alpha+\beta=1$.

Then

$$X=\gamma L^{\alpha}K^{1-\alpha},$$

which can be rearranged to give

$$\frac{X}{K}=\gamma\left[\frac{L}{K}\right]^{\alpha}$$

and taking logs gives

$$\log\left[\frac{X}{K}\right]=\log\gamma+\alpha\log\left[\frac{L}{K}\right].$$

This equation is linear in α, the parameter of interest, and the new variables log (X/K) and log (L/K), which can be readily constructed from data on output, labour and capital.

Difficulty with this procedure arises only when any of the endogenous variables appear both linearly and non-linearly and we require the reduced form, for then the general matrix expression given above does not hold. For example if a price variable P appears on its own, perhaps in an equation explaining price behaviour, and also as the denominator of the ratio Y/P giving in real terms a variable Y which also appears in money terms, then we have three (non-linear) variables given as functions of two endogenous variables, and we cannot write a general (linear) reduced form to cover this situation. If we tried to treat them as three separate variables – Y, P, and Y/P – in obtaining the reduced form, then for given values of exogenous variables and parameters there is no guarantee that the ratio of the reduced form predictions of Y and P is equal to the reduced form prediction of Y/P. If the offending variables were exogenous this problem would not arise. We could just define further exogenous variables as above and it would not matter that pieces of them were appearing in various ways on the right hand side of the reduced form.

2.7 *Stochastic systems*

Exact equations may be convenient for armchair theorising but they do not correspond to observable behaviour. Although definitions, identities, and equilibrium or market-clearing conditions might be thought to hold exactly, we occasionally find quite large 'statistical discrepancies', or 'balancing items'. These will not be our concern, however, – the problem can be avoided by exact measurement. But no exact measurement can ensure that the consumption function fits data on c and y for year after year. While a relationship may fit the data reasonably well over a period of time, or across a cross-section, typically small discrepancies occur year-by-year, or household-by-household. We shall neglect errors of measurement, or 'errors in variables' and concentrate on the random variables, or disturbances, which occur in behavioural relations – 'errors in equations'. These are on the one hand relatively easy to handle but on the other hand difficult to eliminate.

This stochastic element in a behavioural equation is conventionally treated by adding in a random error or disturbance term, u, to give for example $c = \alpha + \beta y + u$. The question arises as to what this new term represents. If we could identify all the variables determining consumption we could conceivably include them in the model. But there are always going to be variables that one cannot identify or measure. The usual rationale is therefore that there are omitted variables in the system whose influence on the dependent variable is represented by the error term. Some of these may only occur once: we may have only one epidemic, international crisis, exceptional summer, change in taste or political incident in our observation period. What happens usually is that there are so many separate unpredictable influences that the sum of them will behave like the random variable which statistical theory is used to handling. One might conceivably invoke the Central Limit Theorem which says that if you have a large number of independent identically distributed random variables, then no matter what their distribution, the distribution of their sum tends to a normal distribution as the number of variables increases. This argument would enable one to claim that the disturbance term has or approximates a normal distribution – an assumption which is useful in certain estimation problems.

We may regard the right hand side of the exact equation discussed earlier as the systematic part of the relationship, and the new element, u, as the non-systematic part. A conventional assumption is that the random variable we add in has a zero mean:

$$E(u) = 0.$$

If the disturbance term has a mean other than zero, then by definition it contains a systematic part, which should be transferred to the intercept or constant term. If $E(u)$ were anything other than zero the difficulty would be that we could not see or identify it, for the mean discrepancy would be indistinguishable from the intercept term, hence the convention of assigning a zero mean value.

To take account of the random error term we need to reinterpret some of the basic concepts introduced earlier. Previously we defined the structure as a complex of features that did not change during a particular observation period and interpreted this for the exact case to cover the form of the equations and specific numerical values of the parameters. Now we must say something about the random error term.

We typically take one of two courses which can be illustrated with an example of a two equation system. The strongest statement about u is made by specifying its probability density function, and when this is done the distribution is typically specified as normal. Our *stochastic structure* might then appear as (specifying the variance of u to be 16)

$$c = 50 + 0.75y + u$$

$$y = c + i$$

$$f(u) = \frac{1}{4\sqrt{2\pi}} e^{-u^2/32}$$

endogenous: c,y
exogenous: i

The last statement might alternatively be written

$$u \sim N(0,16).$$

We have thus used this statement about u to complete the specification of the structure i.e. the form of the equations, the menu of variables, the values of the parameters and the distribution of the random error term. A weaker alternative statement about u is often encountered. The normality assertion is omitted and it is simply specified that (say)

$$E(u) = 0$$

$$E(u^2) = 16$$

i.e. the mean of the disturbances is zero and their variance is 16, but their distribution is left unspecified.

In parallel with the earlier definition, we define a *stochastic model* as a set of stochastic structures. Using the stronger statement about u we can simply write the model by deleting specific values for parameters as follows:

$$c = \alpha + \beta y + u$$

$$y = c + i$$

$$f(u) = \frac{1}{\sigma\sqrt{2\pi}} e^{-u^2/2\sigma^2}$$

endogenous: c,y
exogenous: i

The last statement could alternatively be written as

$$u \sim N(0, \sigma^2).$$

Using the weaker statement about u we would simply write in its place

$$E(u) = 0, E(u^2) = \sigma^2.$$

In a large number of situations this statement is sufficient for estimation purposes and in practice the only occasions on which we really require the stronger statement are in connection with various small sample hypothesis testing procedures. (But remember that the requirement $E(u) = 0$ is not really a restriction at all as we could not distinguish a non-zero mean from the intercept term α).

The number of parameters has been increased by one. They are α, β and σ^2, the variance of the error term. Hence we would describe a change in any of their specific numerical values as a structural change.

The general notation previously discussed can be immediately generalised by adding in the disturbance terms. Illustrating first for the summation notation and adding the error terms on the right hand side we have

$$\sum_{i=1}^{G} \beta_{gi} y_i + \sum_{k=1}^{K} \gamma_{gk} z_k = u_g, \qquad g = 1,\ldots,G$$

where the specification of the model is completed by a statement about the u's, such as that they are joint normally distributed with zero mean. The matrix representation is

$$\mathbf{B\,y} + \mathbf{\Gamma\,z} = \mathbf{u}$$

where $\mathbf{u}$ is a $G \times 1$ column vector. An equation which is an identity is distinguished by an error term which is identically zero, i.e. it is always zero and not just happening to be zero in a particular observation.

The *reduced form* goes through in much the same way as before. From

$$\mathbf{B\,y} + \mathbf{\Gamma\,z} = \mathbf{u}$$

we have

$$\mathbf{B}^{-1}\mathbf{B\,y} = -\mathbf{B}^{-1}\mathbf{\Gamma\,z} + \mathbf{B}^{-1}\mathbf{u}$$

and so

$$\mathbf{y} = \mathbf{\Pi\,z} + \mathbf{v}$$

where Π is as before and $\mathbf{v} = \mathbf{B}^{-1}\mathbf{u}$ is the $G \times 1$ vector of reduced form disturbances. Equivalently we may write

$$y_i = \sum_{k=1}^{K} \pi_{ik} z_k + v_i, \qquad i = 1,\ldots,G.$$

So the reduced form gives each endogenous variable as a linear combination of exogenous variables and structural disturbances. Each reduced form disturbance v_i is in general a linear combination of all the u's, and so we have $E(\mathrm{v}) = 0$; if the u's are normally distributed then so are the v's.

The endogenous variables are now themselves random variables, for in the last equation each y_i is given as a function of v_i, and in the usual prediction exercise we make statements about the conditional mean of their probability distributions (conditional upon the values of the z's, that is). Setting the elements of $\mathbf{v}$ equal to their expected value of zero we simply have

$$E(y_i \mid \mathrm{z}) = \sum_{k=1}^{K} \pi_{ik} z_k, \quad i = 1,\ldots,G.$$

The earlier definition of *exogenous* variables used the idea that they could be regarded as being given from outside the system of equations. In the stochastic case the same idea of exogeneity as relating to determination outside the model requires independence of exogenous variables from all disturbance terms in the model. (In fact this was implicit in the preceding paragraph when we said that the expected value of the v's is zero whatever the values of the z's i.e. $E(\mathrm{v}|\mathrm{z}) = 0$.) So we redefine an exogenous variable as one whose value in any period is independent of the values of all disturbance terms in the model in any period. Thus if z_{kt} denotes the value of the variable z_k in period t, and u_{gt} is the disturbance term in the gth equation in period t, we require z_{kt} and $u_{g,t-l}$ to be independent for all l.

Independence imples zero correlation or covariance (the converse only being true for normally distributed variables) and there may be occasions on which independence is a rather strong assumption, and zero covariance will suffice. Note that since $E(\mathrm{u}) = \mathbf{0}$ the zero covariance requirement can be written as

$$E(z_{kt} u_{g,t-l}) = 0 \qquad \text{for all } l.$$

The exogenous variables in a particular model are typically economic variables themselves, and are presumably determined in some economic system. So long as we can assume that the system which determines them is segmentable from our own model we are free of trouble. However, the notion of segmentability now requires a slight extension. Consider the two systems

$$\mathbf{B}\mathbf{y} + \mathbf{\Gamma}\,\mathbf{z} = \mathbf{u} \qquad\qquad \mathbf{B}^*\mathbf{z} + \mathbf{\Gamma}^*\mathbf{z}^* = \mathbf{w}$$

where the variables which are exogenous in the first system are determined in the second system in terms of other variables z^* and disturbances w. What conditions do we require for exogeneity of the z's in the first system? (i.e. independence of z's and u's)? First, we require the whole thing to be segmentable in the earlier sense – no y variables must appear in the system determining the z's. But second and additionally we require the errors in the z segment (w's) to be independent of the u's. We do not have independence of z's and u's without this mutual independence of the two sets of errors, and this might be hard to achieve in some situations, given the usual omitted variable rationale for both u's and w's.

Let us look at the consequences of these ideas for model-building, starting with our earlier example, which itself begins with the consumption function

$$c = \alpha + \beta y + u.$$

Here we believe that y is not an exogenous variable – it will be correlated with the disturbance term. Why? It may be that the omitted variable rationale can provide some clue, though it is not the main point to be made. Suppose the consumption function was really of the quadratic form we looked at before. Then estimating the function by a linear form will mean that one element thrown into the disturbance term is in fact (say) y^2. As a result one might find a relationship between y and the error term that would repudiate the exogeneity assumption. The practical answer here is to identify as many as possible of the omitted variables.

The main argument for expecting a relationship between y and u i.e. that y is not truly exogenous, is that we have failed to complete the system. The income definition also tells us something about the relationship between c and y. Adding this produces a relationship between y and u because the general reduced form will now relate all endogenous variables to all disturbance terms in the system. Solving

$$c = \alpha + \beta y + u$$

$$y = c + i$$

gives the reduced form

$$c = \frac{1}{1-\beta}(\beta i + \alpha + u)$$

$$y = \frac{1}{1-\beta}(i + \alpha + u)$$

and here we have a statement saying that y depends on u with a positive coefficient ($\frac{1}{1-\beta} > 1$ since $0 < \beta < 1$). Hence y cannot be regarded as exogenous in the consumption function. An upward shift in the consumption function will be associated with a positive increment in income. We have to add an equation to describe this feedback, and this introduces the variable i.

But what if we are now unwilling to accept investment as exogenous? Is i independent of u? Well, in our earlier model i depended on r, the interest rate, and if we now add an error term to this equation, then for i to be exogenous in the two-equation system we require that this error is independent of u. But some investment functions contain income as an indicator of profits, or expected profits; the acceleration principle says that investment is a function of the rate of change of income. So maybe it is difficult to argue that, if u is that bit of consumption unexplained by income, it is independent of investment. Consequently i becomes endogenous, and a further equation is added.

How long must such expansions of the model go on? No matter where we stop someone may always claim that some feedback has been omitted, that our exogenous variables are not truly so and we need more explanatory equations to take account of the implied endogeneity. The practical answer is that if one would only be content with complete independence (or, for the weaker assumption, zero correlations between errors and allegedly exogenous variables) one could hardly stop at all and would end up with a very large system indeed. Therefore some heuristic rule of thumb is required for studies of particular variables or sectors. One must stop when the relationships become negligible, when the fact that the independence assumption is only approximately true has a small influence on the results, and 'small' must be interpreted in the context of the objectives of the particular study. Alternatively, when the analysis is complete, one can check out the basic assumptions that have been made about the behaviour of the errors. If the results are not satisfactory there is no alternative to admitting that a variable previously treated as exogenous can no longer be so regarded, expanding our system, re-estimating and once again checking on the assumptions made.

Exercises

2.1 Verify the reduced form expression given on p.13 for the model presented on p.10.

2.2 Obtain the reduced form of the following supply and demand model, with exogenous y:

demand function:	$q = \alpha_0 + \alpha_1 p + \alpha_2 y + u_1$
supply function:	$q^s = \beta_0 + \beta_1 p + u_2$
market clearing:	$q = q^s$

2.3 Consider the model

$y = c + i + g$	endogenous: y, c;
$c = \alpha + \beta(y - t)$	exogenous: i, g, t.

Suppose that the policy makers choose a target level for y, assign t exogenously, and set g to achieve the target level of y for given i and t. What is the required value of g? Is y now exogenous and g endogenous?

Chapter 3

DYNAMIC SYSTEMS

3.1 *Equilibrium, predetermined variables, final form.*

We now relax the assumption that our model is static but we shall initially assume that the system is exact. Our observations are now over time so that the 'observation period' can no longer refer to a cross-section sample. A system becomes dynamic as soon as the dated variables relate to different time periods, and have links with the past or the future through such mechanisms as trends, incidences of time lags in the structure, rates of change variables, expectations hypotheses or adjustment processes.

We use our dynamic analysis to study the *time path* of variables, or particular properties of the path, in passing from one *equilibrium* position to a new position resulting from some shift in a parameter or exogenous variable. We shall also be interested to examine the equilibrium position from the point of view of its *stability*, i.e. the question of whether once it is attained we stay there. If the system is such that, no matter from what disequilibrium position we start, all time paths of the variables converge to a single equilibrium position, this position is said to be *globally stable.* It is often useful to distinguish this general situation from one which puts restrictions on the starting points which will lead to a stable equilibrium. We shall call an equilibrium position which is reached in the limit from starting points not too far way from it (but which is not reached from all disequilibrium positions) *locally stable.*

The equilibrium position may be static or may itself have dynamic properties – it may be a moving position. For example, in growth models one may talk of the stability of steady state growth – here there is actually an equilibrium path that is achieved by stable systems rather than a single position. So we use the term 'equilibrium' to mean either a point or a path (a set of points).

In discussing the time paths of variables or systems we are interested in *rates of change* of variables. We denote the *first difference operator* by Δ, defined by

$$\Delta x_t = x_t - x_{t-1}$$

This is the discrete time analogue of differentiation with respect to time (i.e. dx/dt, sometimes written $\dot{x}$) which we adopt quite simply because in practice we only have data at discrete intervals. Then what we normally work with is a so-called *difference equation* expressing variables in terms of their levels at points in time and also their rates of change.

We might now write a dynamic consumption function in which consumption depends upon income with a one period lag:

$$c_t = \alpha + \beta y_{t-1}\ .$$

Since $\Delta y_t = y_t - y_{t-1}$, this may also be written $c_t = \alpha + \beta y_t - \beta \Delta y_t$. The first equation is a more precise notation: the second form makes it clear why such equations are called difference equations even though they do not always explicitly contain the first difference operator. The usual identity with time subscripts added completes the model.

$$c_t = \alpha + \beta y_{t-1} \qquad \text{endogenous: } c_t,\ y_t,$$
$$y_t = c_t + i_t \qquad \text{exogenous: } i_t.$$

First, what is the nature of the equilibrium position? Once achieved, the equilibrium values must be continuously maintained, that is, in equilibrium,

$$\ldots = c_{t-1} = c_t = c_{t+1} = \ldots = c^e, \text{ say}$$
$$\ldots = y_{t-1} = y_t = y_{t+1} = \ldots = y^e, \text{ say}$$

(adding a superscript e to denote equilibrium values). These values equally satisfy the above pair of equations, hence we erase time subscripts from the model to look at the equilibrium position as follows:

$$c^e = \alpha + \beta y^e$$
$$y^e = c^e + i$$

(assuming that i_t has a constant value i). We then solve this pair of equations and obtain

$$c^e = \frac{1}{1-\beta}(\alpha + \beta i)$$

$$y^e = \frac{1}{1-\beta}(\alpha + i).$$

Note that this solution is exactly as obtained in the static case (p.4 above). The equilibrium position of the dynamic system has thus been found as the solution of a static model obtained from the dynamic system by erasing the time subscripts.

This statement generalises: for every dynamic system having an equilibrium there is a corresponding static system which describes that position (a simple form of correspondence principle). However, one static system can serve for a number of dynamic systems so that this relationship is not one to one. A simple and trivial illustration of this point is provided in our model, by lagging the income term in the consumption function by two periods, or three periods, and so on. Though each case would provide a different dynamic system the corresponding static system would remain the same.

Now we can ask the second question. Is this equilibrium position attainable? What is the time path?

Let us refer to the starting point as *initial conditions* and denote them by the values y_0 and c_0. The dynamic system then gives the time path of c_t and y_t in terms of initial conditions, parameter values and values of exogenous variables. It is convenient to distinguish the income variable in the two forms in which it appears in this system, y_{t-1} in the consumption function and y_t in the income identity. We call y_{t-1} a *lagged endogenous* variable and y_t (and c_t) *current endogenous* variables. If we are interested in solving the system for the level of the variables at time t the model gives c_t and y_t in terms of y_{t-1} and i_t, that is, current endogenous variables in terms of lagged endogenous and exogenous variables, and these latter are referred to as *predetermined variables.* At time t, the value y_{t-1} is given to us – it is predetermined as of time t. Then the *reduced form* equation for a dynamic system will express current endogenous variables in terms of structural parameters and predetermined variables. Therefore our structural equation for consumption $c_t = \alpha + \beta y_{t-1}$, is already in its reduced form, enabling us to solve for consumption at a point in time in terms of predetermined variables. However it does not tell us what the path of consumption will be over time because y_{t-1} is itself determined in the previous period by the system. We can calculate a solution step-by-step, but we still have to know the path taken by income before we can tell whether the path taken by consumption approaches equilibrium.

To look at the path of consumption we introduce the notion of the *final form* equation which expresses a current endogenous variable in terms of exogenous variables together with lagged values of itself, but of no other endogenous variable. Returning to the consumption reduced form equation we need to get rid of y_{t-1}, which we do by substituting from the income identity, lagged one period:

$$\begin{aligned} c_t &= \alpha + \beta y_{t-1} \\ &= \alpha + \beta c_{t-1} + \beta i_{t-1}. \end{aligned}$$

The last equation, the final form, tells us something about the path taken by an endogenous variable and is independent of the behaviour of all the other endogenous variables – it is a difference equation in only one endogenous variable.

To complete the analysis let us look at the reduced form for income. Substituting for c_t in the income identity gives

$$y_t = \alpha + i_t + \beta y_{t-1} .$$

The point to notice about this reduced form for y_t is that it is already in final form.

How precisely do we find the path taken by our endogenous variables? Clearly what we are looking for is some representation of the time series y_t which we might plot as follows:

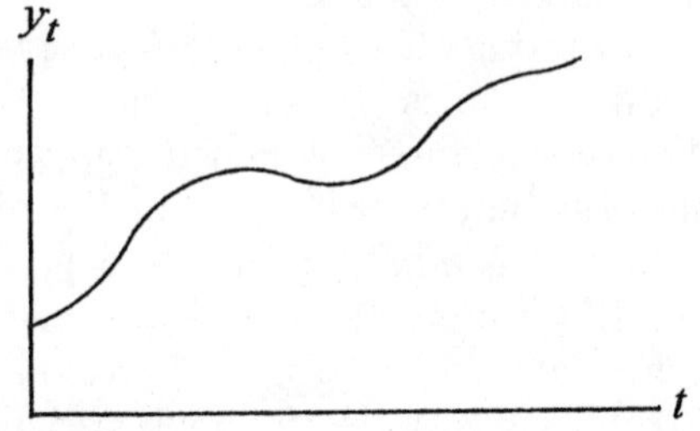

That is, an expression of the endogenous variable as a function of time (and exogenous variables and structural parameters) obtained as the solution of the difference equation.

3.2 *The solution of first order difference equations*

Consider an equation with constant coefficients a and b,

$$y_t = a + by_{t-1}$$

which is said to be of first order because there is only one lag in y in the equation. Suppose we are given the initial condition or starting point, the value y_0 (the intercept on the above diagram). Then the value y_1 is given by the difference equation as

$$y_1 = a + by_0$$

Next, the value y_2 is given by the difference equation as

$$y_2 = a + by_1$$

and substituting from above for y_1 gives

$$y_2 = a + b(a+by_0) = b^2 y_0 + a(1+b).$$

Again, the value y_3 is given by the difference equation as

$$y_3 = a + by_2$$

and substituting for y_2 gives

$$y_3 = b^3 y_0 + a(1+b+b^2).$$

There seems to be a general pattern emerging such that

$$y_t = b^t y_0 + a(1+b+b^2 + \dots + b^{t-1}).$$

Remembering the formula for the summation of a geometric series from earlier schooldays, this expression can be written:

$$y_t = b^t y_0 + a\frac{1-b^t}{1-b} \qquad \text{(assuming } b \neq 1). \qquad (1)$$

Let us conjecture that this is the solution, true for all values of t, and check out the conjecture by substituting back in the difference equation. That is, by asking whether it is true that

$$\left\{b^t y_0 + a\frac{1-b^t}{1-b}\right\} = a + b\left\{b^{t-1} y_0 + a\frac{1-b^{t-1}}{1-b}\right\}$$

Well, the term $b^t y_0$ cancels out on both sides, and what remains on the right hand side can be written

$$a\frac{1-b}{1-b} + a\left\{\frac{b(1-b^{t-1})}{1-b}\right\} = a\frac{1-b^t}{1-b}$$

which is equal to the remaining term on the left hand side, and so the equation holds and our solution is confirmed.

In the case b=1, the geometric series summation cannot be used, but the solution (1) can in this case be written

$$y_t = y_0 + at.$$

The difference equation is in this case $y_t = a + y_{t-1}$ and the solution is easily confirmed, for

$$(y_0 + at) = a + [y_0 + a(t-1)].$$

Thus we have derived a relationship between y and time giving the path of y, assuming that we know the starting point. (Those who have previously studied difference equations will recognise the above as an example of a particular solution, given in terms of a specific starting value y_0.) In order to see whether this path converges to the equilibrium value, we can arrange the solution in a more informative way. The equilibrium value y^e is given in our simple illustration by

$$y^e = a + b\,y^e, \qquad \text{i.e. } y^e = \frac{a}{1-b},$$

whereupon the solution can be written

$$y_t = b^t y_0 + (1-b^t)y^e$$

$$\text{or} \qquad y_t - y^e = b^t(y_0 - y^e).$$

Thus y_t will approach y^e if and only if the right hand side goes to zero as t increases, and this requires $b^t \to 0$ as $t \to \infty$ (assuming that the system didn't actually start out in equilibrium, with $y_0 = y^e$). The necessary and sufficient condition for $b^t \to 0$ is $|b| < 1$, which gives us the *stability condition.* So, in this first order case, whether a dynamic system converges to an equilibrium depends on the magnitude of the coefficient of the lagged dependent variable in the final form difference equation. If $|b| < 1$, the values y_t approach the equilibrium value y^e; if $|b| > 1$, the system diverges or explodes. If $b < 0$, the path is oscillatory; if $b > 0$, the path is smooth or monotonic. If $b = 1$, y_t has a linear trend ad infinitum; if $b = -1$, y_t oscillates around y^e with constant amplitude.

Returning to our model, the final form equation for income was

$$y_t = \alpha + i_t + \beta y_{t-1}$$

and assuming that $i_t = i$, constant over time, we had obtained the equilibrium position as

$$y^e = \frac{1}{1-\beta}(\alpha + i)$$

Now we know that the solution for y_t is

$$y_t = \beta^t y_0 + (\alpha+i)\frac{1-\beta^t}{1-\beta},$$

$$\text{or} \qquad y^t - y^e = \beta^t(y_0 - y^e).$$

(You should check that the final form and equilibrium value for consumption yield a solution of identical form, viz.

$$c_t - c^e = \beta^t(c_0 - c^e).)$$

The stability condition is $|\beta| < 1$, and we expect to have a stable solution since β is the mpc. We may sketch the two convergent situations as follows, assuming that $y_0 < y^e$. (The assumption that i_t is constant implies a fixed equilibrium value y^e; if we were to specify that i_t varied over time in some way, following a linear trend say, then the equilibrium position would be a moving one, and the path of y_t would approach this equilibrium path rather than the horizontal line in the diagram.)

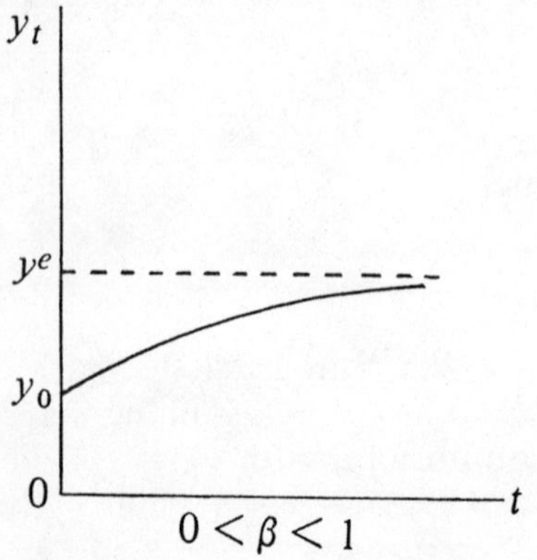

$0 < \beta < 1$

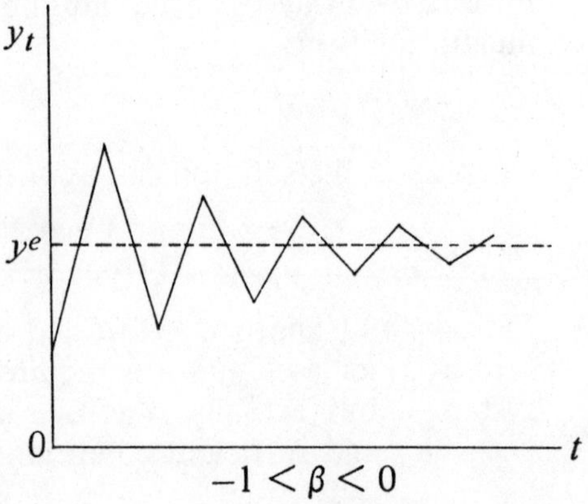

$-1 < \beta < 0$

3.3 *Further examples of dynamic models*

Let us now illustrate the proposition that, while there exists a corresponding static model describing an equilibrium position for every dynamic model, nevertheless the same static model can serve for more than one dynamic model. The static three equation model is as follows:

$$y = c + i \qquad \text{endogenous: } y,\ c,\ i$$
$$c = \alpha + \beta y \qquad \text{exogenous: } g$$
$$i = \gamma y + g$$

Investment now depends on income, and has an exogenous component g. We develop two simple examples of dynamic systems.

Example 1

We first retain the consumption function of the preceding sections in which consumption depends on income with a one period lag:

$$c_t = \alpha + \beta y_{t-1}.$$

The model is completed by adding the remaining two equations with current dated variables:

$$y_t = c_t + i_t$$
$$i_t = \gamma y_t + g.$$

It is simpler to assume that g_t has a constant value g say, so that there is a single equilibrium position given as a function of g rather than a moving equilibrium position which is a function of g_t. Substituting into the income identity gives

$$y_t = \alpha + \beta y_{t-1} + \gamma y_t + g$$

and on rearranging we obtain the reduced form for income

$$y_t = \frac{\alpha+g}{1-\gamma} + \left[\frac{\beta}{1-\gamma}\right] y_{t-1}.$$

The reduced form equation is already in final form: it contains no lagged endogenous variables other than lagged values of y_t, the dependent variable. The first term is what we called a in our discussion of the solution of difference equations; the term in square brackets is what we were calling b. Hence the solution for y_t in terms of an initial condition y_0, the values α, β, γ, g, and time could be easily though rather messily written out.

Turning to questions of stability we see that in this example the stability condition is

$$-1 < \frac{\beta}{1-\gamma} < 1.$$

If this holds then the system is stable, and converges towards the equilibrium position obtained as the solution of the static model.

What is meant by getting a stability condition for the whole system by looking at the final equation for y_t? Could we not instead have derived the final equation for c_t and the final equation for i_t, which are equally endogenous variables of the model, to get a stability condition of the model? It turns out that the autoregressive structure of the final equation – the way the dependent variable depends on its own past – is the same for every endogenous variable in the model. You can check that the final equations for c_t and i_t contain the single lagged value c_{t-1} and i_{t-1} respectively, in each case with the above square bracketed coefficient, but the rest of the equation will not generally be the same. Hence we only need to look at the final equation of any one endogenous variable to obtain the stability condition of the model.

The above inequality can be manipulated to study the stability condition further. We require

$$-1 < \frac{\beta}{1-\gamma} < 1.$$

If $1-\gamma > 0$ (i.e. $\gamma < 1$) then this becomes

$$-(1-\gamma) < \beta < 1-\gamma.$$

f $1-\gamma < 0$ (i.e. $\gamma > 1$) then we have

$$-(1-\gamma) > \beta > 1-\gamma,$$

remembering that multiplying through an inequality by a negative number reverses the direction of the inequalities. The admissible pairs of values of β and γ satisfying the stability condition can now be obtained, and illustrated in the following diagram, stable solutions being given by pairs of values lying in the shaded area.

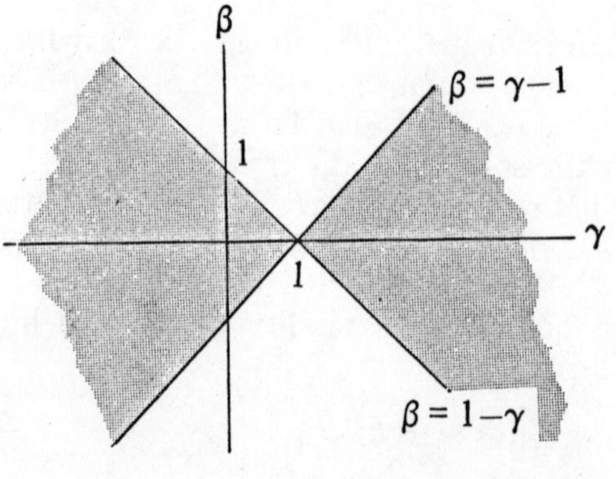

The boundaries between pairs of values satisfying the inequality and those not satisfying it are obtained by replacing the inequality by an equality. Thus whether γ is greater than or less than 1, these boundaries are the lines $\beta = \gamma - 1$ and $\beta = 1 - \gamma$. The shaded area is obtained by examining simple points such as (γ=0, β=0) and (γ=2, β=0), and checking that they satisfy the inequalities, whereas points such as (γ=1, β=±1) do not. Having derived the stability conditions we may postulate that the system *is* stable so that we can deduce restrictions on the sets of parameter values which are admissible. It might well be that we only want to look at the positive quadrant. If we assume that $0 < \beta < 1$ then the operative restriction is $\beta + \gamma < 1$ if $\gamma < 1$.

Example 2

A second dynamic example illustrates both that one can use a given static system to represent equilibrium positions for more than one dynamic system and again that restrictions on parameter values may be derived from the requirements of stability. We revert to an unlagged consumption function and assume that current investment depends on last period's income, so our model is now

$$\begin{aligned} y_t &= c_t + i_t \\ c_t &= \alpha + \beta y_t \\ i_t &= \gamma y_{t-1} + g \end{aligned}$$

endogenous: y_t, c_t, i_t

exogenous: g.

The reduced form equation for y_t is

$$y_t = \frac{1}{1-\beta}(\gamma y_{t-1} + \alpha + g),$$

which is already in its final form. The stability condition is therefore

$$-1 < \frac{\gamma}{1-\beta} < 1.$$

If $1-\beta>0$, we require

$$-(1-\beta) < \gamma < 1-\beta,$$

while if $1-\beta<0$, the inequality becomes

$$-(1-\beta) > \gamma > 1-\beta.$$

Following the same procedure as before gives a diagram in which the shaded area represents pairs of values yielding stable solutions.

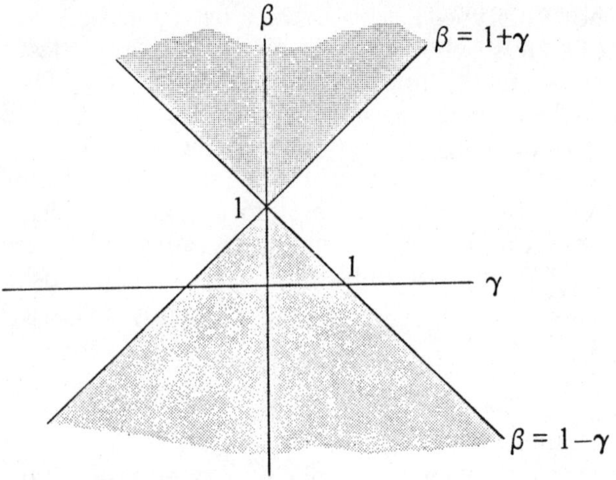

Again, postulating the system's stability, we can derive restrictions on the coefficients of the original model. If it is assumed that $0<\beta<1$, then the effective restriction for positive values of γ is once more $\beta+\gamma<1$.

Thus, having observed a stable real world, the stability conditions give values of parameters which are, a priori, reasonable. It then becomes an empirical question as to whether an estimated system in fact satisfies these restrictions. If one comes up with point estimates outside the range of values satisfying the stability condition, then the usual conclusion is that one's estimated system does not adequately represent the real world. So an examination of the stability implications of an estimated dynamic system provides a validation procedure for that system.

3.4 *Distributed lag mechanisms*

One can gain an impression from reading the empirical literature that distributed lag equations represent all of dynamics as they are currently somewhat fashionable. Their basic idea is that one variable reacts to another over a period of time rather than at a given instant. Formally, y reacts to x with a *distributed* lag if y_t is some function of x_t and its past values, $y_t = f(x_t, x_{t-1}, \ldots,)$, or in linear form

$$y_t = \beta_0 x_t + \beta_1 x_{t-1} + \beta_2 x_{t-2} + \ldots = \sum_{j=0}^{\infty} \beta_j x_{t-j}$$

A *fixed* lag of k periods would be one where y_t depended only on x_{t-k}, and the case k=0 represents instantaneous response. We may illustrate a possible adjustment of y to a new equilibrium value following a maintained increase or step in x at time t_0 as follows:

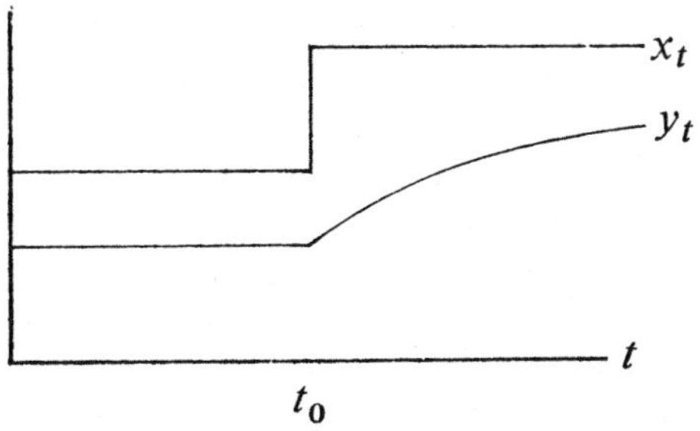

The maximum lag in the system can of course be fixed but it is often taken to be infinity for mathematical convenience. Nonetheless we would expect that at least after the passage of some periods the β_j begin to decline and of course we require that the sum of the β's converges to a finite limit.

The β's are sometimes called *reaction coefficients* because they describe the reaction of y to a unit shock (or unsustained change) in x j periods earlier. We can represent this as follows:

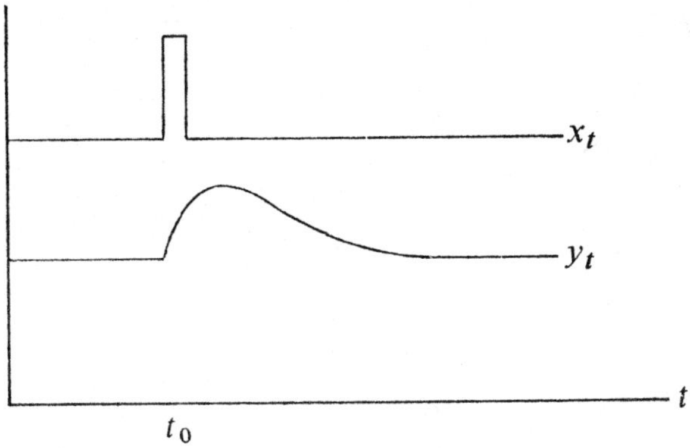

In this diagram the displacement of y from its long-run level is given at time t_0+j by the coefficient β_j. In the earlier diagram where the change in x was maintained, the change in y after j periods is given by the partial sum $\sum_{i=0}^{j} \beta_i$, and the complete sum $\sum_{i=0}^{\infty} \beta_i$ gives the *total multiplier*. In either case we can refer to β_0 as the *impact multiplier*. If the β's are all positive, β_j may be regarded as the weight attached to the lag of length j, and an *average lag* may be calculated as the weighted average $\dfrac{\Sigma j\beta_j}{\Sigma \beta_j}$

In some situations we may put stronger restrictions on the β's, as well as requiring them to go to zero as j becomes large. For example, we might require the sum of the β-coefficients to be one. This would happen, for instance, if the y-variable was housing completions and the x-variable housing starts. The distribution of the β_j's would then be precisely the same as the distribution of construction times: a house that takes eight months to construct appears in the completions data eight months after it has appeared in the starts data. If the construction time is not fixed but has some frequency distribution then that distribution will emerge exactly in the distribution of the β_j's. One would impose $\Sigma\beta_j = 1$ on the assumption that houses once started, get completed.

The Koyck simplification

The general form $y_t = \Sigma\beta_j x_{t-j}$ is practically useless for empirical work, for there are as many coefficients as observations. We reduce the number of parameters by postulating some general form describing the behaviour of the β_j's. The simplification introduced by Koyck in his work *Distributed Lags and Investment Analysis* (1954) has had a substantial impact, for it leads to a regression equation which can be readily estimated, and has also been shown to have a meaningful interpretation in terms of economic behavioural hypotheses, as discussed in the next section.

Koyck assumed that, after some point, the coefficients decline *geometrically*. We may not wish to specify how the first few β_j's behave, but the simplest form (which is a perfectly good illustration of the technique) is obtained if we assume that the geometric decline does start at the beginning. Then we have

$$\beta_j = \lambda^j\beta, \qquad j=0,1,\ldots, \qquad 0<\lambda<1$$

where β is some constant and the requirement that λ is between 0 and 1 ensures that the β_j's converge smoothly to zero. The vastly simplified distributed lag equation, containing only two parameters, is

$$y_t = \beta\sum_{j=0}^{\infty}\lambda^j x_{t-j}.$$

The impact multiplier, measuring the instantaneous effect of x on y, is given by β, and the total multiplier, measuring the change in the equilibrium value of y caused by a unit increase in the level of x, is

$$\Sigma\beta_j = \beta\Sigma\lambda^j = \frac{\beta}{1-\lambda}.$$

The average lag is

$$\frac{\beta \Sigma j \lambda^j}{\beta \Sigma \lambda^j} = \frac{\lambda}{1-\lambda} \cdot$$

It may seem that this restriction has not got us very far because the infinite past of the x series still appears on the right hand side. Here Koyck introduced a very neat trick which gives a directly estimable equation. The equation at time t is

$$y_t = \beta(x_t + \lambda x_{t-1} + \lambda^2 x_{t-2} + \lambda^3 x_{t-3} + \ldots)$$

and if we lag the equation by one period and multiply both sides by λ we have

$$\lambda y_{t-1} = \lambda\beta(x_{t-1} + \lambda x_{t-2} + \lambda^2 x_{t-3} + \ldots)$$

$$= \beta(\lambda x_{t-1} + \lambda^2 x_{t-2} + \lambda^3 x_{t-3} + \ldots).$$

Now we see that the terms on the right hand side of the latter equation correspond to terms, other than the first, on the right hand side of the y_t equation. So if we subtract one from the other everything but one term (βx_t) cancels, giving

$$y_t - \lambda y_{t-1} = \beta x_t.$$

The infinite past of the x-series has disappeared, and we have a final equation yielding direct estimates of β and λ from a finite sample of data:

$$y_t = \lambda y_{t-1} + \beta x_t.$$

(Similar results are obtained if the original distributed lag equation has an intercept term:

$$y_t = \alpha + \beta \sum_{j=0}^{\infty} \lambda^j x_{t-j}.$$

Then, repeating the above argument, the final equation is

$$y_t = \alpha(1-\lambda) + \lambda y_{t-1} + \beta x_t$$

which is again readily estimable, and the value of α can be deduced from the values of the constant term $\alpha(1-\lambda)$ and the coefficient λ.)

3.5 *Adaptive expectations and partial adjustment*

Now we consider what sort of behaviour by economic agents might give rise to these distributed lags.

Let us first assume that behaviour with respect to a particular dependent variable is influenced by expected or anticipated values of some explanatory variable. The expectations might relate to such variables as sales, prices, incomes or interest rates according to the particular problem in hand. For example, a retailer's inventories may depend on the sales he expects to make in the following period, money balances may react to expected interest rates, consumption to expected income, raw material stocks to expected prices, and so on. Then there are typically three ways in which economists proceed.

First, actual observations on the expectational variables might be available from, say, surveys on sales anticipations or business investment intentions. These are relatively rare, however, and in most cases anticipations remain unobservable.

A second possibility is to set up hypotheses about the outcome of the forecasting procedure. For example, one might say that the forecast level of a variable turns out to be some average of actual present and past values:

$$\hat{X}_t = \rho X_{t-1} + (1-\rho)X_t$$

where the hat denotes the expected value of a variable. Such a descriptive statement would not say anything about the mechanism by which anticipations or intentions are formed, but would only be a representation of its outcome. With $0 < \rho < 1$, expected changes have a systematic tendency to underestimate actual changes [i.e. $\hat{X}_t - X_{t-1} = (1-\rho)(X_t - X_{t-1})$], this effect, called the 'regressiveness' of expectations, having been observed when anticipations data were compared with actual values of the variable, after the event. At one extreme, if $\rho=0$, it is assumed that the variable is accurately forecast, and that the actual variable may be used as a proxy for the anticipated variable. If $\rho=1$ we have the static or naive expectations model, in which last period's conditions are expected to prevail.

The adaptive expectations hypothesis

A third approach to expectational variables is to make a specific assumption concerning the mechanism by which expectations are formed. The adaptive expectations hypothesis is an example of such an assumption which has seen successful application in empirical work. It was first applied in the mid-fifties by Phillip Cagan in his study of hyperinflation and by Marc Nerlove in his study of the dynamics of agricultural supply. It appeared shortly thereafter in Milton Friedman's theory of the consumption function.

The hypothesis states that expectations are amended or adapted in proportion to past forecasting errors. The forecast level of a variable in the next period ($\hat{x}_{t+1}$) is given by the forecast of the current level ($\hat{x}_t$) amended by some proportion of the current forecasting error ($x_t - \hat{x}_t$). Thus

$$\hat{x}_{t+1} = \hat{x}_t + (1-\gamma)(x_t - \hat{x}_t)$$

or

$$\hat{x}_{t+1} = \gamma\hat{x}_t + (1-\gamma)x_t, \qquad \text{with } 0 \leq \gamma < 1. \qquad (1)$$

Hence the hypothesis is that the expectations will only be amended or adapted if they are incorrect. If expectations underestimate we increase them; if they overestimate we reduce them.

The hypothesis has been applied in alternative formulations differing in two respects. First, Cagan's formulation was in a continuous time model: he used a differential rather than our difference equation. Secondly, in some formulations the relative timing of expectations and actual values is changed, and the hypothesis is written

$$\hat{x}_t = \hat{x}_{t-1} + (1-\gamma)(x_t - \hat{x}_{t-1}).$$

This version possibly results from Cagan's formulation where one is only considering infinitesimally small time intervals, and the distinction between the two forms is negligible. This formulation may also be more appropriate in applications devoid of a specific forecasting context, such as Nerlove's work, where the hypothesis is used to derive the 'normal price' appearing in the agricultural supply function, and Friedman's work on the consumption function, where expected income (estimated permanent income) is formed in this way from actual income data. However, equation (1) may be intuitively clearer with its direct operational meaning, for the next period's forecast is calculated in terms of this period's actual value which, it is assumed, has been already observed: this is the formulation we shall adopt. But it is a straightforward exercise to show that altering the time subscripts does not change any of the substantive conclusions, and the reader is asked to bear these alternative interpretations in mind.

Examining the way in which expectations depend on the actual past values by repeated substitution, we have

$$\begin{aligned}
\hat{x}_{t+1} &= (1-\gamma)x_t + \gamma\hat{x}_t \\
&= (1-\gamma)x_t + \gamma\,[(1-\gamma)x_{t-1} + \gamma\hat{x}_{t-1}] \\
&= (1-\gamma)x_t + \gamma\,(1-\gamma)x_{t-1} + \gamma^2\,[(1-\gamma)x_{t-2} + \gamma\hat{x}_{t-2}] \\
&= \ldots \\
&= (1-\gamma)\sum_{j=0}^{\infty} \gamma^j x_{t-j}.
\end{aligned}$$

(The effect of the remote expectation term $\hat{x}_{t-r}$ dies away, for its coefficient γ^{r+1} goes to zero as r increases, since $0 < \gamma < 1$). A value of γ close to zero imples that the coefficients $(1-\gamma)\gamma^j$ decline rapidly as j increases, and so expectations depend on rather recent experience: in the original version (1), the actual value x_t is weighted more heavily than $\hat{x}_t$. When γ is close to 1, actual values from the more distant past enter the expectations formula, current information being discounted more heavily: in this situation we see from (1) that expectations are slow to change.

The expression for $\hat{x}_{t+1}$ in terms of an infinite distributed lag on x_t with geometrically declining coefficients is thus a direct consequence of the adaptive expectations hypothesis, but is precisely the simplified form of distributed lag considered in the previous section. So if we postulate a behavioural relationship

$$y_t = \alpha + \beta \hat{x}_{t+1}$$

(where y_t might be inventories and $\hat{x}_{t+1}$ forecast sales) with expectations formed by

$$\hat{x}_{t+1} = \gamma \hat{x}_t + (1-\gamma)x_t$$

then by substituting in for $\hat{x}_{t+1}$ we are back in the Koyck framework

$$y_t = \alpha + \beta(1-\gamma) \sum_{j=0}^{\infty} \gamma^j x_{t-j}.$$

And the Koyck transformation (subtract the equation lagged one period and multiplied by γ) can be applied to eliminate the infinite past of x_t and give the estimating equation

$$y_t = \alpha(1-\gamma) + \beta(1-\gamma)x_t + \gamma y_{t-1}.$$

This form in which expectations are generated appears also in the operations research literature under the guise of exponentially weighted moving averages (cf. Holt, Modigliani, Muth, and Simon *Planning Production, Inventories and Work Force*) and in some situations this is advocated as a way of actually forecasting. Note again that though it is generated by weighting all past observations with increasing powers of γ, it is very economical in calculation, for we need not remember the infinite past of the series but just the current observations and the current forecast, in order to apply (1). The procedure can be generalised to incorporate trend and seasonal effects.

Partial adjustment or stock adjustment hypotheses

The duality we shall now demonstrate was first noticed by Nerlove and followed hard on the heels of the development of the adaptive expectations hypothesis.

Suppose we have a desired level of some variable (y_t^*) and this depends on an explanatory variable x_t as follows:

$$y_t^* = \alpha + \beta x_t.$$

But assume that there are frictions, delays, costs of doing business, habit persistence, such that the desired level is never entirely achieved in a single period. The actual change in y from the previously existing level $(y_t - y_{t-1})$ is only some fraction of the change required to achieve the desired level $(y_t^* - y_{t-1})$. Assuming the proportion achieved is $(1-\gamma)$, where $0 < \gamma < 1$, the partial adjustment hypothesis can be written

$$y_t - y_{t-1} = (1-\gamma)(y_t^* - y_{t-1}).$$

or

$$y_t = (1-\gamma)y_t^* + \gamma y_{t-1}.$$

Small values of γ imply relatively quick adjustment, and vice versa. At the extremes, if $\gamma = 0$ we have instantaneous adjustment and if $\gamma = 1$ nothing ever changes.

If we now take the original expression for the (unobserved) desired level in terms of explanatory variables, and substitute into the partial adjustment equation, we immediately have

$$y_t = \alpha(1-\gamma) + \beta(1-\gamma)x_t + \gamma y_{t-1}.$$

This is precisely the same final equation as that obtained from the adaptive expectations hypothesis and shows the duality between the partial adjustment and adaptive expectations hypotheses. Thus if we find that a regression equation of this form provides a satisfactory explanation of y_t, it is still open to argument whether lags in adjustment or expectational variables are at work. Regression analysis cannot distinguish the two hypotheses. Even though we have not had to apply the Koyck transformation to get the partial adjustment final form, the hypothesis can with perfect equivalence be restated as a distributed lag equation in x_t with coefficient declining exponentially by repeated substitution for the lagged y term.

Again, we might calculate an average lag as $\gamma/(1-\gamma)$. Alternatively we might wish to calculate how long it would be before some proportion of the desired adjustment is achieved, given that adjustment is never fully complete if $0 < \gamma < 1$ (although we may of course be close to 100% adjustment after a relatively short period.) How do we calculate the number of periods for adjustment to be a given proportion (p) complete?

After one period $(1-\gamma)$ of the change is accomplished, so γ of the change is remaining. In the second period, $(1-\gamma)$ of this is eliminated so after two periods a total of $(1-\gamma) + \gamma\,(1-\gamma) = (1-\gamma^2)$ is accomplished and γ^2 remains. By the end of the third period $(1-\gamma)$ of this is achieved and γ of it remains, i.e. γ^3 of the original desired change remains. In general we have that after n periods

$$1 - \gamma^n$$

of the desired change is accomplished. If we set this expression equal to some value p we may solve for n to give us the number of periods required for adjustment to be a proportion p complete:

$$p = 1-\gamma^n$$

therefore
$$n = \frac{\log(1-p)}{\log \gamma}$$

As an illustration let us ask when the change will be 90% complete (p=0.9) for various values of γ. If $\gamma = 0.1$ (actual change is 0.9 of the desired change) then the number of periods required is of course one. If $\gamma = 0.5$, then the number of periods required is

$$n = \frac{\log 0.1}{\log 0.5} = 3.32.$$

If $\gamma = 0.9$ (a high value of the coefficient of the lagged dependent variable, implying slow adjustment) we have

$$n = \frac{\log 0.1}{\log 0.9} = 21.8.$$

In many of the empirical studies which use this formulation, the estimated coefficient of y_{t-1} does indeed turn out to be relatively large, although we shall see that there may be purely statistical reasons for this. If such an equation is estimated from quarterly data, a coefficient of 0.9 implies that five and a half years are required for a desired changed to be 90% complete – quite a drag. Results of this kind with respect to the demand for money, for example, have led monetary economists to believe that the system reacts rather slowly, whether the delays are caused by expectations which are slow to adapt or adjustment which is very partial.

3.6 *Dynamic stochastic theory*

It is now necessary to combine the elements of previous sections and consider a model that is both dynamic and stochastic. We will consider the consequences of doing so for some of the simple definitions we have introduced.

We begin by adding an error term to a dynamic equation. Using the dynamic consumption function equation as an illustration gives

$$c_t = \alpha + \beta y_{t-1} + u_t,$$

or, in the case of the partial adjustment hypothesis,

$$y_t = (1-\gamma)y_t^* + \gamma y_{t-1} + u_t.$$

The addition of the error term is analogous to what we did in discussing static stochastic equations. In the above equation giving a stochastic formulation of the partial adjustment hypothesis, for example, we are saying that the level of y_t is not simply determined by partial adjustment to some desired level, but also there are a host of other omitted variables that we cannot see or identify influencing y_t, and these are lumped together in the error term u_t.

The general form goes through in much the same way as in the static case

$$\sum_{i=1}^{G} \beta_{gi}y_{it} + \sum_{k=1}^{K} \gamma_{gk}z_{kt} = u_{gt}, \qquad g = 1,...,G.$$

Not only have we added the error term here, but every variable now has a time subscript, and the z's are predetermined in the earlier sense (p.23), a definition which will be to some extent modified for the dynamic stochastic case in a moment. They include lagged endogenous variables and exogenous variables. Sometimes a notation is used that distinguishes the two types so that lagged endogenous variables are written specifically as $y_{i,t-l}$ and truly exogenous variables are denoted by x_{jt}. Note that in determining the grand total K of predetermined variables every lagged value of an endogenous variable is counted separately. In matrix notation the general form can be written:

$$\mathbf{B}\mathbf{y}_t + \mathbf{\Gamma}\mathbf{z}_t = \mathbf{u}_t,$$

where $\mathbf{y}_t = (y_{1t},...,y_{Gt})'$, $\mathbf{z}_t = (z_{1t},...,z_{Kt})'$, and $\mathbf{u}_t = (u_{1t},...,u_{Gt})'$

To complete the structure we need a statement about the u's such as that they are joint normally distributed or that they have particular covariance properties. And we might also add a statement or assumption about serial dependency (which we return to below). The two important aspects to distinguish are contemporaneous covariances between different elements of the vector $\mathbf{u}_t$ and autocovariance of a single u_{gt} with its own past. At a given point in time we might expect correlations among different elements of the vector

$$\begin{bmatrix} u_{1t} \\ u_{2t} \\ \cdot \\ \cdot \\ \cdot \\ u_{Gt} \end{bmatrix}$$

since some of the omitted variables might be common to different equations: this usually presents no difficulty. Over time, we might also observe autocorrelation in a single disturbance term, that is, a correlation of u_{gt} with $u_{g,t-1}$, $u_{g,t-2}$, ... as we shall see, this presents rather more difficulty.

The reduced form now becomes

$$y_{it} = \sum_{k=1}^{K} \pi_{ik} z_{kt} + v_{it} \qquad i = 1,\ldots,G,$$

or $$\mathbf{y}_t = \Pi \mathbf{z}_t + \mathbf{v}_t$$

and gives each current endogenous variable in terms of variables which are predetermined as of time t, and disturbance terms. The final form equations as before contain no lagged endogenous variables other than lagged values of the dependent variable. The general derivation is very messy and is not presented here.

We can now return to the definition of a *predetermined variable* in stochastic dynamic systems. An exogenous variable was introduced as a variable determined outside the system of equations, and in the stochastic case was required to be independent of all the errors in the model in all time periods. If we attempt to apply the same requirement to lagged endogenous variables in generalising this definition to cover predetermined variables we come unstuck, for it is no longer possible to obtain independence of all the errors in the model at all periods of time. For example, at time t, y_{t-l} is a lagged endogenous or predetermined variable, but it is determined at time $t-l$ as a function of u_{t-l}, among other things. So we cannot require independence of past errors. What we do require is independence between z_t and current and future disturbances. Hence we adopt a final modification of our definition: a variable z_t is *predetermined* at time t if it is independent of all current and future disturbances in the model ($\mathbf{u}_t$, $\mathbf{u}_{t+1}$, $\mathbf{u}_{t+2}$,...,). An equivalent formulation would define a predetermined variable as one whose past values were independent of the current disturbance terms $\mathbf{u}_t$. So it does not really matter whether we look at a given value of z_t at a particular time and current and future values of the u's or at a given value of u_t and previous values of the predetermined variable.

Suppose we have a two equation system containing a consumption function with a current and lagged income term and the usual income identity. (We return to the alphabetic representation of variables, and as there is only one error term in the model, we write it u_t with no other subscripts).

$$c_t = \alpha + \beta_1 y_t + \beta_2 y_{t-1} + u_t \qquad \text{endogenous: } c_t,\ y_t,$$
$$y_t = c_t + i_t \qquad \text{exogenous: } i_t.$$

Then the question is what do we assume about these variables? The usual exogeneity assumption for i_t is no different – we require its independence of...,u_{t-1},u_t,u_{t+1},... . But y_{t-1} must be independent of $u_t, u_{t+1}, u_{t+2}, \ldots$ to be predetermined at time t. It is not independent of u_{t-1}, for we have

$$c_{t-1} = \alpha + \beta_1 y_{t-1} + \beta_2 y_{t-2} + u_{t-1}$$
$$y_{t-1} = c_{t-1} + i_{t-1}.$$

Hence we can see how y_{t-1} is determined in terms of u_{t-1} via the consumption function – the reduced form equation for y_{t-1} includes u_{t-1}.. Suppose that u_t is independent of its own past values u_{t-1}, u_{t-2}, ...: then although y_{t-1} depends on u_{t-1}, it will be independent of u_t, and can be regarded as a predetermined variable as of time t. If this is not satisfied, however, and u_t is correlated with u_{t-1}, then y_{t-1} and u_t will be correlated via their common link with u_{t-1}, and y_{t-1} fails to be predetermined. So for a lagged endogenous variable to be regarded as predetermined we need the error term to be independent of its past values, that is, to be free of autocorrelation. (Note that the term 'serial correlation', which in some strict definitions refers to correlation between one variable and lagged values of another variable, is often used for 'autocorrelation', which refers to the correlation between a variable and lagged values of itself.)

The above definition of a predetermined variable is the same as that to be found in the text by C. F. Christ and it is worth noting that not all authors go as far as this in the requirements for predeterminacy. Some are satisfied simply that a predetermined variable be either exogenous (with the usual definition) or lagged endogenous. The consequence of this less strict definition, ignoring questions of the behaviour of the errors as it does, is that one regards these questions of autocorrelation of the error term as separate. The question of autocorrelation becomes an empirical one rather than a matter of the assumptions governing the nature of the economic variables in the model.

By working out a simple example, let us see why, if u_t is not independent of its own past, lagged endogenous variables may fail to be predetermined in this strict sense. Stripping the problem down to its bare essentials, we have

$$y_t = \beta y_{t-1} + u_t$$
$$u_t = \rho u_{t-1} + \epsilon_t,$$

where ϵ_t is independent of its own past and future. In this case the error term u is assumed to follow a simple first order autoregression: it depends upon its own past. Here we can evaluate the covariance of u_t and y_{t-1} to demonstrate that y_{t-1} cannot be regarded as predetermined by the strict definition above. The covariance $E[u_t - E(u_t)]\,[y_{t-1} - E(y_{t-1})]$ is equal to $E(u_t y_{t-1})$ by the assumption that $E(u_t) = E(\epsilon_t) = 0$. By simple substitution from the second equation and from the first equation lagged one period we have

$$E(u_t y_{t-1}) = E(\rho u_{t-1} + \epsilon_t)(\beta y_{t-2} + u_{t-1})$$
$$= \rho\beta E(u_{t-1} y_{t-2}) + \rho E(u_{t-1}{}^2) + \beta E(\epsilon_t y_{t-2}) + E(\epsilon_t u_{t-1})$$

after multiplying out. Since ϵ_t is, by assumption, independent of its own past it is independent of the past values of anything else in the model (i.e. u_t depends on ϵ_t, and u_{t-1} depends on ϵ_{t-1}, but if ϵ_t and ϵ_{t-1} are uncorrelated, so will be ϵ_t and u_{t-1}) and the last two expected values are zero. The first term in the last line contains the covariance of a u-value with a y-value one period earlier, just as on the left hand side, but it is measured at time $t-1$, not at t. However, if we make the conventional assumption of 'stationarity' (that covariance properties are constant over time), these two expected values are the same. Equally, $E(u_{t-1}{}^2)$ and $E(u_t{}^2)$ are then equal, giving just the variance of u. (In this model, stationarity is provided by the requirement that $|\beta|<1$, $|\rho|<1$, – cf. Exercise 3.6). So the equation becomes

$$E(u_t y_{t-1}) = \rho\beta E(u_t y_{t-1}) + \rho E(u_t{}^2)$$

i.e.

$$E(u_t y_{t-1}) = \frac{\rho \text{var}(u)}{1-\rho\beta}$$

Now this covariance is zero only if ρ is zero and so it is only in that case that y_{t-1} satisfies our strict definition of a predetermined variable. And of course a zero value of ρ implies that u_t is non-autocorrelated.

Exercises

3.1 Obtain the reduced form and final equation for y_t, and the stability condition for the following model:

$$c_t = \alpha + \beta y_t + \gamma c_{t-1}$$
$$y_t = c_t + i_t$$
i_t exogenous.

3.2 Obtain the final equation for y_t and the stability condition for the following model:

$$c_t = \alpha + \beta y_t$$
$$y_t = c_t + i_t$$
$$i_t = \gamma \Delta y_t + g_t$$
g_t exogenous.

3.3 Suppose that the desired level of y depends on next period's forecast value of x:

$$y_t^* = \alpha + \beta \hat{x}_{t+1}$$

where $\hat{x}_{t+1} = \gamma \hat{x}_t + (1-\gamma) x_t$.

The actual level of y adjusts to the desired level according to

$$y_t - y_{t-1} = (1-\lambda)(y_t^* - y_{t-1}).$$

Obtain an equation expressing y_t as a function of a finite number of observed values of x and y. From estimates of this equation, could you obtain separate estimates of γ and λ? What is the implication of your answer? (cf. the discussion on p.37).

3.4 Consider the market for a commodity which is produced in an annual crop. The quantity demanded depends on the current price, whereas the quantity supplied this year is a function of last year's price; the market is cleared in every year.
(a) Set up a system of linear equations to describe the behaviour of this market. Under what conditions is the system stable?
(b) Now suppose that the quantity supplied is a function of this year's expected price, where price expectations are formed according to the adaptive expectations hypothesis. Show that, for certain values of the adaptive expectations parameter, this change will stabilize a previously unstable system.

3.5 Adding a disturbance term u_t to the consumption function, derive the final equation for c_t in stochastic versions of the models in Exercises 3.1 and 3.2. Check that in each case the final equation for c_t has the same autoregressive structure as that for y_t (note the discussion on p.28). In each case, is the lagged dependent variable independent of the error term in the final equation?

3.6 Consider the first order autoregression

$$u_t = \rho u_{t-1} + \epsilon_t$$

where ϵ_t has mean zero and variance σ^2 for all t, and is independent of ϵ_{t-l} for $l \neq 0$. In terms of the parameters ρ and σ^2, obtain expressions for
(a) the variance of u_t
(b) the correlation between u_t and u_{t-1}
(c) the correlation between u_t and u_{t-2}
(d) the correlation between u_t and u_{t-l}
Are your answers true for all values of ρ?

3.7 Consider the simple structural equation

$$y_t = \beta y_{t-1} + u_t$$

where u_t is given by

$$u_t = \alpha u_{t-2} + \epsilon_t$$

the periods representing seasons, say summer and winter. Evaluate the covariance between u_t and y_{t-1}.

Chapter 4

THE IDENTIFICATION PROBLEM

4.1 *Introduction*

Let us first recap some earlier discussion to put the identification problem in context. We said that a priori economic theorising can tell us very little about the actual magnitudes of the parameters of behavioural relations, and that estimation of the structural parameters is necessary if we wish to test hypotheses about the underlying behaviour or simply to obtain numerical values as ends in themselves. On the other hand, if all we are interested in is prediction, then there is a case in which we do not need to know structural parameters at all, and the sequence we follow is:

data → *reduced form coefficients* → *predictions of endogenous variables*

This is valid when there is no intervening change of structure between the observation and prediction periods (pp.4-5 above) (although we shall in due course find a situation in which knowledge of the structural parameters improves the predictions even in the absence of structural change). In the presence of structural change, however, we need to know or estimate the parameters of behavioural relationships in the observation period, so that the effect of the change can be assessed before moving to predictions, and the sequence is as follows:

data → *(1) reduced form coefficients* → *(2) 'old' structural parameters* → *(3) 'new' structural parameters*
→ *(4) new reduced form coefficients* → *(5) predictions of endogenous variables*

Knowledge of the structural change is incorporated at stage (3), and stages (4) and (5) are straightforward algebraic operations as discussed in sections 2.2 and 2.5. Stages (1) and (2) will be our concern for the remainder of this book. Whether stage (2) is possible, that is, whether numerical values of structural parameters can be deduced from a given (estimated) reduced form is the *identification* problem, and the *estimation* problem arises at stage (1). The identification problem is logically prior, and is treated first, because if it is not possible to infer structural parameter values from reduced form coefficient values, there is no point in estimating the reduced form (except for prediction under unchanged structure). Although the estimation problem is presented here as the problem of obtaining reduced form coefficient estimates from data on the endogenous and exogenous variables during the observation period, we shall see in the next chapter that there are ways of estimating the structural parameters directly from the data, provided that the model is identified (i.e. that stage (2) is possible). So even here it is necessary to check the identifiability of the model (or its equations, or their parameters) before attempting any estimation.

To concentrate attention on the identification problem we shall assume in this chapter that we have perfect knowledge of the reduced form and that such stage (1) problems as sampling variability in estimates can be ignored. One way of looking at this is to assume that we have an infinite sample of data. Thus we collapse the first link in the above chain, and use 'data' and 'reduced form' as equivalent concepts.

The identification problem arises because there may be a number of structures that will generate the same reduced form, or the same observations. Equivalently, given a set of data, many hypotheses could be formulated to account for the observations. What we attempt to do is to eliminate as many of these hypotheses as possible on a priori grounds, arguing that they are inconsistent with economic theory, and the identification problem is solved when exactly one hypothesis (or structure) remains which is consistent with both data and theory. The most common way in which a priori restrictions are imposed on a general relationship as a result of theoretical reasoning is by specifying particular values for parameters – typically we specify that a parameter is zero if the theory leads us to believe that the variable to which the parameter is attached does not influence the particular economic behaviour in question. Here we shall not be considering situations in which the theory leads to statements concerning the behaviour of the error terms, and so we shall proceed by considering the exact equivalents of the stochastic models we are interested in analysing. That is, we consider that the 'data' give us a perfectly known exact reduced form.

To introduce a more formal treatment, we call the set of structures that are consistent with the data the *data-admissible* structures. For an equation to be consistent with the data we mean that the given set of z-values and the corresponding y-values given by the reduced form satisfy the equation exactly. Recall that the use of the term 'structure' implies that numerical values of parameters are specified (p.3). Thus the data-admissible structures are those whose reduced forms are identical (having identical coefficient values) with the given data or reduced form. Koopmans* speaks of structures in a data-admissible set being 'observationally equivalent.'

Somewhat more trivially, the set of structures consistent with the model, obeying the restrictions imposed by the model, are said to be *model-admissible.* To go back to our earliest example on p.2, any equation that contains only consumption and income and excludes investment is model-admissible as a consumption function: it satisfies the restrictions of the theory.

We can now use these two notions to define exactly what we mean by identifiability. A *structure* is *identified* with respect to a given model and given data if there is one and only one structure that is both model- and data-admissible: i.e. there is only one set of numerical values of the structural parameters corresponding to the reduced form given by the data that also satisfies the prior restrictions imposed by the model. This definition can be disaggregated to apply to the identifiability of a single structural equation or even of a single parameter value. Thus, again, a structural equation is identified if there are unique values of its parameters corresponding to the given reduced form and satisfying the prior restrictions. We may have a model in which some equations are identified and other equations are not. Similarly some parameter values of a single equation in a model may be identified while other parameter values are not. (One example of an under-identification situation arose in the discussion of distributed lag models. Since an adaptive expectations hypothesis and a partial adjustment hypothesis both resulted in the same final form, even perfect estimation would not enable us to distinguish the two hypotheses. Cf. Exercise 3.3, where γ and λ are not identified.)

4.2 *A supply-demand illustration.*

Case 1. Let us start with a very simple form of a supply-demand model. The supply and demand equations say that the quantities supplied and demanded are functions of the price of a commodity.

*Tjalling C. Koopmans, "Identification Problems in Economic Model Construction," Chapter II of *Studies in Econometric Method* eds. W. C. Hood and T. C. Koopmans, (Cowles Commission Monograph 14), Wiley; 1953.

We ignore the error terms as noted above, and substitute $q = q^s = q^d$ from the market clearing condition, and so have:

$$D: \quad q = \alpha_0 + \alpha_1 p \qquad \alpha_1 < 0$$
$$S: \quad q = \beta_0 + \beta_1 p \qquad \beta_1 > 0$$

We are interested in the numerical values of the parameters and let us suppose that someone in the Treasury knows what the actual parameter values are. He then takes the demand equation and multiplies it by some constant (say $\frac{3}{5}$) and the supply equation by another ($\frac{2}{5}$) and adds them together. He claims that the resulting equation

$$D': \quad q = \frac{3\alpha_0 + 2\beta_0}{5} + \frac{3\alpha_1 + 2\beta_1}{5} p,$$

is the demand equation, and no econometrician could discover what had happened from the data. Similarly, he might multiply the demand equation by $\frac{1}{3}$ and the supply equation by $\frac{2}{3}$ add the two together and call the result a supply equation.

$$S': \quad q = \frac{\alpha_0 + 2\beta_1}{3} + \frac{\alpha_1 + 2\beta_1}{3} p.$$

This might even be published in *Economic Trends*. The point is that there would be no data which could reveal what our deceitful Treasury economist had done provided that the restrictions imposed by the theory were still met. They would then be

$$\frac{3\alpha_1 + 2\beta_1}{5} < 0, \quad \frac{\alpha_1 + 2\beta_1}{3} > 0,$$

and so long as these hold the deceit is undetected.

The original demand and supply equations are not identified: they have the same reduced form as the equations that are derived as linear combinations of them. Thus data satisfying D and S will also satisfy D' and S' because both pairs of equations have the same reduced form. Moreover D' and S' also satisfy the restrictions imposed by the model (i.e. if $\frac{3\alpha_1 + 2\beta_1}{5} < 0$ and $\frac{\alpha_1 + 2\beta_1}{3} > 0$). We have more than one set of model admissible equations that satisfy the data. Hence the model is not identified.

An early paper on this subject is that by Working*, who observed that with the above pair of demand and supply curves no set of data

*E. J. Working, "What Do Statistical 'Demand Curves' Show?" *Quart. J. Econ.*, 1927. Reprinted in A.E.A. *Readings in Price Theory*, pp. 97-115.

will enable us to pick out a relation which we can call the demand curve and a relation which we can call the supply curve. Even if we have errors in each equation all the data will lie around the intersection of the two curves and we shall not be able to obtain separate demand and supply relations:

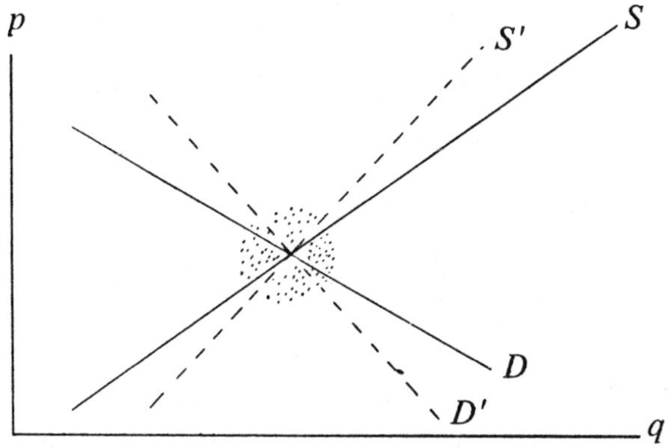

Working observed, however, that if one curve shifts systematically while the other remains fixed, then the p–q observations given by the intersections of the curves will all lie on the curve which does not shift, which is hence identified. This gives us our next case.

Case 2. We now introduce income into the demand function:

$$D: \quad q = \alpha_0 + \alpha_1 p + \alpha_2 y \qquad \alpha_1 < 0; \alpha_2 > 0$$
$$S: \quad q = \beta_0 + \beta_1 p \qquad \beta_1 > 0$$

We expect that demand depends negatively on price and positively on income. If this structure (with specific numerical values for α's and β's) generates the data, then the p, q and y observations will also satisfy any linear combination of these equations. Hence we can obtain sets of data admissible equations simply by taking linear combinations of the equations. Let us now be slightly more general by multiplying the demand equation by $(1-h)$ and the supply equation by h, where $0 \leq h \leq 1$. Now we can say that

$$q = [(1-h)\alpha_0 + h\beta_0] + [(1-h)\alpha_1 + h\beta_1]p + (1-h)\alpha_2 y$$

is a data-admissible equation. (It does not necessarily define the entire set of data-admissible equations but it does contain a good number of them.) Is this a model admissible equation as a supply curve or as a demand curve or as neither? We know it fits the data. Next we must decide whether we can pass it off as a particular equation of the model.

It certainly cannot do as a supply equation because it contains income, and our model says that supply does not depend upon income. There is only one special case in which the equation would look like a supply equation according to the restriction and that is when $h = 1$ and income is excluded. But this gives the original supply equation, and so we conclude that it is identified: there is one and only one equation which is both data admissible and model admissible as the supply equation.

When $h \neq 1$ the equation certainly could be the demand equation (because it would then contain income with a positive coefficient), provided that the price coefficient remained negative,

$$\text{i.e. } (1-h)\alpha_1 + h\beta_1 < 0.$$

This implies a restriction on h, namely that

$$0 \leqslant h < \frac{\alpha_1}{\alpha_1 - \beta_1}$$

However, with α_1 negative and β_1 positive there are many values of h satisfying this restriction. There are therefore lots of data admissible equations that satisfy the restrictions imposed by the theory and are thereby model-admissible as the demand equation, which is therefore not identified.

In terms of the simple diagrammatic representation used in Working's 1927 paper we are saying that we have a supply equation relating p and q but, for every different income level, we have a different demand equation. As income varies the demand curve in the $p-q$ plane shifts and the observations on p and q will lie along the supply curve which is thereby identified.

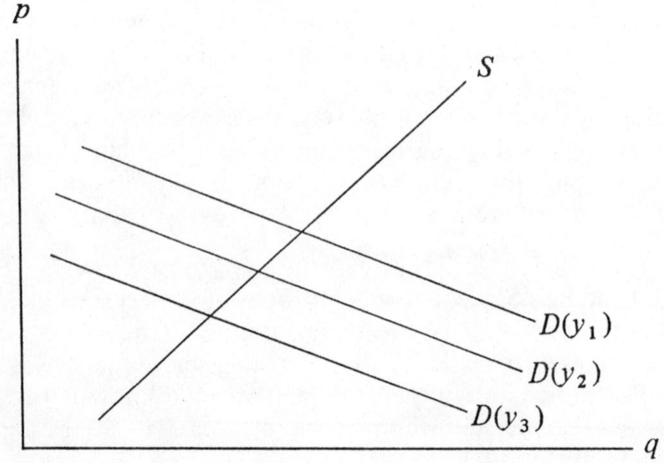

Case 3. We can identify the demand curve similarly i.e. by a shifting supply curve. A model in which this is true is

$$D: \quad q = \alpha_0 + \alpha_1 p$$
$$S: \quad q = \beta_0 + \beta_1 p + \beta_3 w$$

where w might be the wage rate or the weather. Again, there is no linear combination of the two equations that satisfies the restriction imposed on the demand curve, that is, that excludes w. In this situation the p–q data obtained as w varies show us the demand curve, which is thereby identified.

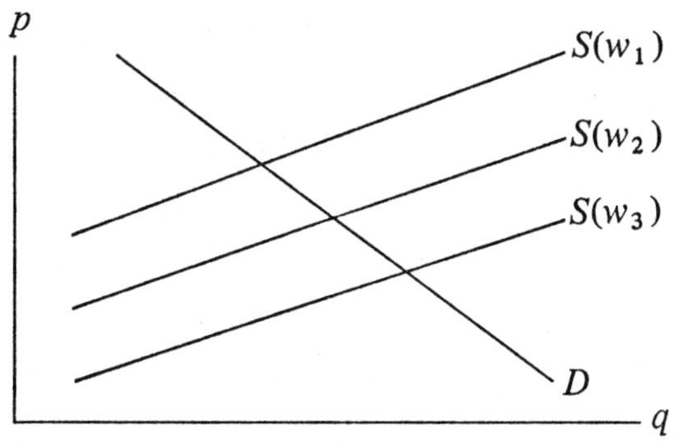

Case 4. Putting the last two cases together we can take a final case where both demand and supply curves shift.

$$D: \quad q = \alpha_0 + \alpha_1 p + \alpha_2 y$$
$$S: \quad q = \beta_0 + \beta_1 p \qquad\qquad + \beta_3 w$$

In this case of course we cannot readily represent the situation diagrammatically as the observations in the price and quantity plane will not lie on any particular curve. But this fact tells us nothing about identification. Let us set up a data admissible linear combination of the supply and demand structure equations and see whether it is model admissible in each case. Multiplying the demand equation by the proportion $(1-h)$ and the supply equation by h and summing the results gives the following equation satisfying the data:

$$q = (1-h)\alpha_0 + h\beta_0 + [(1-h)\alpha_1 + h\beta_1]p + (1-h)\ \alpha_2 y + h\beta_3 w$$

However no general equation of this kind can satisfy the restrictions of the model. Only if $h = 1$, so that income is excluded, is the restriction on the supply equation satisfied, and only if $h = 0$, so that w is excluded, can the equation serve as a demand equation. But these cases give the supply and demand functions themselves and so both are identified – in each case there is one and only one equation that satisfies both the data and the restrictions imposed by the theory.

So we begin to see that an equation is made identifiable by the *exclusion* of one variable from it, and the specification of a zero coefficient that we spoke about in discussing general notation (p.11) appears to have some purpose. Any equation that includes all the variables appearing in the model is unidentified. If we were to construct a fifth case by putting y and w into both demand and supply equations then they would both have the same form and neither would be identified.

We began this chapter by saying that identification is necessary for us to be able to calculate structural parameters from reduced form parameters. Let us return to this question in terms of these illustrations. Take the example of case 4. The two endogenous variables are p and q, with y and w exogenous, and the reduced form is

$$p = \frac{\beta_0 - \alpha_0}{\alpha_1 - \beta_1} - \frac{\alpha_2}{\alpha_1 - \beta_1} y + \frac{\beta_3}{\alpha_1 - \beta_1} w$$

$$q = \frac{\alpha_1\beta_0 - \alpha_0\beta_1}{\alpha_1 - \beta_1} - \frac{\alpha_2\beta_1}{\alpha_1 - \beta_1} y + \frac{\alpha_1\beta_3}{\alpha_1 - \beta_1} w.$$

Using a generalised representation for reduced forms, we may write

$$p = \pi_{10} + \pi_{11} y + \pi_{12} w$$
$$q = \pi_{20} + \pi_{21} y + \pi_{22} w$$
$$\left(\text{where } \pi_{10} = \frac{\beta_0 - \alpha_0}{\alpha_1 - \beta_1} \text{ etc.}\right)$$

Now we assume that actual numerical values of the π's are given to us and ask whether we can work back to the actual numerical values of the structural parameters, α's and β's. In this particular case, of course, we expect that we can do so because we have already established that both demand and supply equations are identified.

Beginning with α_1. Since $\pi_{12} = \dfrac{\beta_3}{\alpha_1 - \beta_1}$ and $\pi_{22} = \dfrac{\alpha_1\beta_3}{\alpha_1 - \beta_1}$ it is clear that $\alpha_1 = \dfrac{\pi_{22}}{\pi_{12}}$, so that given the numerical values of π_{12} and π_{22} we can get that of α_1. We can derive all other structural parameter values in the same way. It is worth checking out the following results:

$$\alpha_0 = \pi_{20} - \frac{\pi_{22}}{\pi_{12}} \pi_{10}, \qquad \alpha_1 = \frac{\pi_{22}}{\pi_{12}}, \qquad \alpha_2 = \pi_{21} - \frac{\pi_{11}\pi_{22}}{\pi_{12}}$$

$$\beta_0 = \pi_{20} - \frac{\pi_{21}}{\pi_{11}} \pi_{10}, \qquad \beta_1 = \frac{\pi_{21}}{\pi_{11}}, \qquad \beta_3 = \pi_{22} - \frac{\pi_{12}\pi_{21}}{\pi_{11}}$$

In an unidentified system we will not be able to solve out all the structural parameters that appear in the model. In case 2 considered above (p.49) the supply curve did not shift (w was absent), but the demand function did (as a function of y). We can represent that situation in our present model by setting $\beta_3 = 0$ so that the wage variable disappears from the model. The reduced form would then simply have p and q as a function of one exogenous variable, y:

$$p = \pi_{10} + \pi_{11}y$$
$$q = \pi_{20} + \pi_{21}y$$

These four reduced form coefficients are the same functions of the α's and β's as above; setting $\beta_3 = 0$ simply implies $\pi_{12} = \pi_{22} = 0$. Now we have five structural parameters and only four reduced form coefficients which necessarily means that will not be able to deduce unique values of α's and β's from given π-values. This model therefore cannot be identified. Let us see in what sense this is so. The equations we want to solve are

$$\pi_{10} = \frac{\beta_0 - \alpha_0}{\alpha_1 - \beta_1} \qquad \pi_{11} = \frac{-\alpha_2}{\alpha_1 - \beta_1}$$

$$\pi_{20} = \frac{\alpha_1\beta_0 - \alpha_0\beta_1}{\alpha_1 - \beta_1} \qquad \pi_{21} = \frac{-\alpha_2\beta_1}{\alpha_1 - \beta_1}$$

Again we see immediately that $\beta_1 = \frac{\pi_{21}}{\pi_{11}}$ and the equation for β_0 still holds, hence the supply equation remains identified. Now what about the α's? Let us try to solve the π_{11} and π_{21} equations for α_1 and α_2, using the already determined value for β_1:

$$\pi_{11} = \frac{\alpha_2}{\beta_1 - \alpha_1} \qquad \pi_{21} = \frac{\alpha_2\beta_1}{\beta_1 - \alpha_1}$$

therefore $\pi_{11}\left(\frac{\pi_{21}}{\pi_{11}} - \alpha_1\right) = \alpha_2$ therefore $\pi_{21}\left(1 - \frac{\alpha_1}{\pi_{21}/\pi_{11}}\right) = \alpha_2$

i.e. $\pi_{21} - \pi_{11}\alpha_1 = \alpha_2$ i.e. $\pi_{21} - \pi_{11}\alpha_1 = \alpha_2$

– the same relation between α_1 and α_2 results, so the next step of solving for α_1 and α_2 is not possible.

All we have is a linear relation between α_1 and α_2 which can be satisfied by a large number of values. Similarly the π_{10} and π_{20} equations both give

$$\alpha_0 = \pi_{20} - \alpha_1\pi_{10}.$$

Thus we have two equations in three unknowns and the demand equation is not identified. Although there is an infinite range of values of α_0, α_1 and α_2 satisfying these two equations once any one of them is specified the other two follow immediately. For example, if we could specify a particular value for the income elasticity of demand (α_2) from somewhere beyond our model, α_0 and α_1 would follow. Effectively, then, we are short of just one piece of information, or one restriction, without which the demand function is unidentified.

4.3 *General considerations; order and rank conditions*

Returning now to the general formulation, recall that we said that we could form a set of data-admissible equations by taking linear combinations of the true structure equations (with the correct parameter values specified, that is). We now argue for the general linear model both that any linear combination of the structure equations is data admissible and also that no linear equation that is not formed in that way is data admissible. On the one hand this is a useful general way of forming sets of data-admissible equations and on the other it gives *all* the data admissible equations. We begin with the now familiar general form

$$\sum_{i=1}^{G} \beta_{gi} y_i + \sum_{k=1}^{K} \gamma_{gk} z_k = 0 \qquad g=1,\ldots,G$$

(continuing to work with the exact case for convenience). Each of these equations, with specified β- and γ-values, is true for every set of observed y- and z-values. It remains true when multiplied through by some constant h_g, and when all equations, multiplied by constants $h_1, h_2, \ldots, h_G$, are added, we still get an equation that is satisfied by the y_i and z_k values. So when we take linear combinations with weights h_g, all resulting equations remain data-admissible. (Of course, if only one such weight, say h_j, is non-zero, then we get the jth structure equation back again).

Now what we need to show is that any linear equation satisfying the data must in fact be obtained in this way. Suppose the following linear equation fits the data

$$\sum_{i=1}^{G} \alpha_i y_i + \sum_{k=1}^{K} \delta_k z_k = 0.$$

The reduced form $y_i = \sum_{k=1}^{K} \pi_{ik} z_k$, $i=1,\ldots,G$ is unique (assuming det $\mathbf{B}$ is non-zero), and the numerical values of the π's are given by the data. Thus, these are the only expressions for y_i satisfying the data. So if the previous equation satisfies the data it must be obtained by taking α_1 times the first reduced form equation plus α_2 times the second equation plus α_3 times the third, and so on. That is, it must be a linear combination of reduced form equations. But each reduced form equation is itself a linear combination of the structure equations (constructed so as to eliminate all y's but one). Hence any linear equation satisfying the data must be a linear combination of the true structure equations.

This helps quite a bit, because it means that we need only consider equations that are linear combinations of the true structural equations in the model. The problem then becomes whether such an equation is model-admissible as one of the structural equations, in the sense that it satisfies the restrictions imposed by the model. Let us continue to assume for the time being that the only restrictions we have to deal with are zero restrictions. Then what we need to check is whether any linear combinations of the structure equations contain exactly the same variables as the structural equation of interest, no more, no less. If so, then the structural equation is not identified, for there is more than one data-admissible equation satisfying the exclusion restrictions.

Proceeding in small steps, we now consider a three-equation example, based on a model of joint demand for two commodities. We get by with only three equations by assuming that the supply of one of the commodities is given and completely inelastic.

$$\begin{array}{lll} D \text{ for good 1:} & q & = \alpha_0 + \alpha_1 p + \alpha_2 p' + \alpha_3 y \\ S \text{ of good 1:} & q & = \beta_0 + \beta_1 p \qquad\qquad + \beta_4 w \\ D \text{ for good 2:} & q' & = \gamma_0 + \gamma_1 p + \gamma_2 p' + \gamma_3 y \end{array}$$

endogenous: q,p,p', exogenous: y,w.

q and p are the quantity and price of the first good, an equilibrium condition $q^s = q^d = q$, say, having been substituted in. For the second good, with price p', the quantity q' is fixed – supply is inelastic. (We could alternatively represent this by regarding the third equation as an equation for q'^d, and adding a fourth equation $q'^s = \delta_0$ (constant) and a market clearing condition $q'^s = q'^d = q'$ – after substitution, however, the net effect is the same.) We now ask are these equations identified, or are there linear combinations of the equations of identical form?

First, look at the supply equation. It will be identified if there is no linear combination of the other equations which excludes both p' and y. To exclude p' we have to form a linear combination of the two demand equations with weights in inverse proportion to the coefficients on p', i.e. γ_2 times the D_1 equation less α_2 times the D_2 equation will give us a linear combination that will exclude p'. What about y? We can similary exclude it with weights inversely proportional to the coefficients on y, i.e. γ_3 times the D_1 equation less

α_3 times the D_2 equation yields an equation from which income has disappeared. But can we exclude both p' and y at the same time? If we cannot do so we can say that the supply equation is identified. We cannot exclude both unless the weights we have established above turn out to be the same in both cases so that excluding p' will automatically exclude y and vice versa. This will happen if the weights are in the same proportion i.e. if $\frac{\gamma_2}{\alpha_2} = \frac{\gamma_3}{\alpha_3}$. If this equation establishing proportionality among the required weights is not true then it will be impossible to establish a linear combination (which would also include S_1) that 'looks like' the supply equation, which is thereby identified. Hence we have in practice established an identifiability condition in terms of some coefficients appearing in the other equations of the model, namely those on variables excluded from the equation whose identifiability is in question. Unless $\alpha_2\gamma_3 - \alpha_3\gamma_2 = 0$ the supply equation is identified. Such an absolute equality is extremely unlikely and the possibility would in practice be ignored. Nonetheless this condition must in principle be satisfied for this first equation to be identified. An alternative expression of this identifiability condition is that

$$\begin{vmatrix} \alpha_2 & \alpha_3 \\ \gamma_2 & \gamma_3 \end{vmatrix} \neq 0.$$

What of the first equation? It excludes w so its specification cannot be matched by a linear combination which includes the supply equation, for this would introduce w. But any linear combination which has a zero weight for equation S_1 and is thus based only on D_1 and D_2 will exclude w, and will therefore be of the same form as D_1 (remember q' is a constant). Hence D_1 is not identified.

Now look at the third equation. It is worth your checking that it is identified.

Let us conjecture that a general rule is emerging. In the two equation model we found that for an equation to be identified it must exclude at least one variable appearing in the model. In the three equation example one exclusion is not enough, at least two variables must be excluded for identifiability. Indeed, there is a general rule – the *order condition* for identifiability:

In a model of G linear equations, to be identified an equation must exclude at least $G-1$ of the variables appearing in the model.

(We typically distinguish between a 'just identified' equation, from which exactly $G-1$ variables are excluded, and an 'overidentified' equation, which excludes more than $G-1$ variables.) However, this is by no means the whole story. One might guess that the order condition is necessary but not sufficient, for in the above three equation case the supply equation satisfied the order condition but we also required a particular two-by-two determinant to be non-zero. This suggests that we can state a condition for identifiability that is both necessary and sufficient in terms of the appropriate determinant. This gives us the *rank condition*:

> *In a linear model of G equations, an equation is identified if and only if at least one non-zero $(G-1) \times (G-1)$ determinant is contained in the array of coefficients with which those variables excluded from the equation in question appear in the other equations.*

If the rank condition is satisfied the order condition must also be satisfied, but not vice versa, so the order condition is necessary but not sufficient. (Recall that the rank of a matrix is the order of the largest non-zero determinant that it contains.)

Our procedure in applying the rank condition to a system would be, first, to inspect a particular equation and see what variables of the model, either endogenous or exogenous, are excluded from it. We then look at the coefficients on those excluded variables in the remaining equations. That array will certainly have $G-1$ rows because there are obviously that number of other equations in the system. How many columns will the array of excluded coefficients have? It will be the same as the number of excluded variables. There cannot, for example, be a $(G-1) \times (G-1)$ non-zero determinant if there are fewer than $(G-1)$ variables excluded. In our previous example the array of excluded coefficients was

$$\begin{bmatrix} \alpha_2 & \alpha_3 \\ \gamma_2 & \gamma_3 \end{bmatrix}$$

It has $G-1 = 2$ rows because there are three equations in the system. Are there two or more columns? Yes, as the order condition is satisfied.

As a final example, let us take one more step and construct a four equation model. (Again, we have been aligning variables in columns so that the system can be quickly written in matrix form, preserving our columns of coefficients with zeros in places where variables are excluded.) We make q' endogenous, inserting a supply function for the second good, and collect all terms on one side.

$$\begin{aligned}
D_1&: -q \quad\quad + \alpha_0 + \alpha_1 p + \alpha_2 p' + \alpha_3 y \quad\quad\quad\quad = 0 \\
S_1&: -q \quad\quad + \beta_0 + \beta_1 p \quad\quad\quad\quad\quad\quad + \beta_4 w = 0 \\
D_2&: \quad\quad -q' + \gamma_0 + \gamma_1 p + \gamma_2 p' + \gamma_3 y \quad\quad\quad\quad = 0 \\
S_2&: \quad\quad -q' + \delta_0 \quad\quad\quad + \delta_2 p' \quad\quad\quad\quad\quad\quad = 0
\end{aligned}$$

There are four endogenous variables (q,q',p,p'), two exogenous variables (y,w), and the constant terms which can be regarded as the coefficients of a third exogenous variable which is always one. We can write out the elements of the B and Γ matrices side by side to simplify matters, the column heading indicating the variable to which a column of coefficients is attached.

	q	q'	1	p	p'	y	w
D_1:	-1	0	α_0	α_1	α_2	α_3	0
S_1:	-1	0	β_0	β_1	0	0	β_4
D_2:	0	-1	γ_0	γ_1	γ_2	γ_3	0
S_2:	0	-1	δ_0	0	δ_2	0	0

Let us check out the order condition. We count the variables excluded from each equation by counting the zeros in each row, and compare with $G-1 = 3$.

	No. of zeros	*Order condition*
D_1:	2	not identified
S_1:	3	just identified
D_2:	2	not identified
S_2:	4	over identified

The provisional conclusions are given above. Where the verdict is that an equation is not identified the provisional conclusion is also the final one. This is because, as we have said, fulfilment of the order condition is necessary for identification. It is impossible that we should find the first and third equations identified using the rank condition.

Applying the rank condition to the second equation we get the following array of coefficients of excluded variables (i.e. q',p',y):

$$\begin{bmatrix} 0 & \alpha_2 & \alpha_3 \\ -1 & \gamma_2 & \gamma_3 \\ -1 & \delta_2 & 0 \end{bmatrix}$$

Since the equation is only just identified by the order condition this array has only three columns, the minimum necessary for identification. Is the matrix of rank three, i.e. does it contain a 3 X 3 non-vanishing determinant? The determinant is

$$\alpha_3(\gamma_2-\delta_2)-\alpha_2\gamma_3.$$

Unless this is zero (and there is no reason to believe that it is) the equation is identified. If this determinant proved to be zero it would of course mean that there was a linear combination of these three equations which would exclude q', p' and y. We may in practice be able to sign elements in this expression on the basis of a priori reasoning, but of course we will not know the actual numerical values. Nevertheless, it is extremely unlikely that this function of the five parameters would turn out to be zero, and so we proceed on the assumption that it is not and therefore the rank condition is satisfied. (It may be possible, after estimation, to construct a statistical test of such hypotheses.)

There is no point in looking at the rank condition for the third equation as the relevant coefficient array is 3 X 2, and certainly cannot contain a non-zero 3 X 3 determinant – the failure to satisfy the order condition indicates lack of identification. Equivalently, note that any linear combination of the last two equations excludes q and w, and so obeys the restrictions of the D_2 equation.

The relevant array of coefficients for the fourth equation is

$$\begin{bmatrix} -1 & \alpha_1 & \alpha_3 & 0 \\ -1 & \beta_1 & 0 & \beta_4 \\ 0 & \gamma_1 & \gamma_3 & 0 \end{bmatrix}$$

Does this matrix have rank 3? We can get four 3 X 3 determinants, and so long as we are willing to assert that any one of them is non-zero, we are home and dry. One of the 3 X 3 determinants is obtained by dropping the second column, and is $\gamma_3\beta_4$. We have assumed a priori that neither of these coefficients is zero, and so the rank condition is satisfied. (Note that if $\beta_4 = 0$, so that w disappears from the model, there is still a non-zero determinant in the first three columns. In this case, this equation ceases to be over-identified and becomes just identified.)

In many situations the rank condition will in this way merely underline the order condition for we usually simply assume that it is safe to proceed as if the relevant function of structural parameters were non-zero. But there are cases where it will throw up a different answer – there are examples of this in Exercises 4.1 and 4.2.

Identities and identification

We have made no mention so far of the treatment of identities in the context of identifiability of parameter values, equations, and structures. Indeed our illustrative models have not contained identities. There are two possibilities. We shall see that they can be treated by substituting them in to the other equations of the system (and so reducing the number of equations and variables) but this usually introduces restrictions on the remaining coefficients, the correct treatment of which we shall have to consider. Alternatively identities can be left in the equation system. In that case there is no question of identification involved since the coefficients of an identity are, by definition, fully specified a priori and the data satisfy the equation period by period automatically (typically coefficients are specified to be 1 or −1). Though one can disregard their own identification, they must be included for such matters as counting up the number of variables and equations – identities are counted among the G equations in case they are not substituted into other equations.

An equivalent order condition

Now we return to the general linear form

$$\sum_{i=1}^{G} \beta_{gi} y_i + \sum_{k=1}^{K} \gamma_{gk} z_k = 0 \qquad g = 1,\ldots,G$$

continuing with the exact case, and with a priori information expressed in terms of zero restrictions in the parameters. From considering this general case we can state the order condition for identification in a slightly more usable form. Let us suppose that the gth equation is under consideration, and some of the β_{gi} and γ_{gk} are specified to be zero. In looking at the order condition we have so far made no distinction between endogenous and predetermined variables. Let us now separate these out, and say that in the gth equation H endogenous variables appear, so that $G–H$ are excluded or have zero coefficients, and that J predetermined variables are included, so that $K–J$ z-variables are excluded. We may renumber the endogenous variables so that the included variables are the first ones $(y_1,\ldots,y_H)$ and the excluded ones are the remainder $(y_{H+1},\ldots,y_G)$. Similarly the predetermined variables appearing in the structural equation are $z_1,\ldots,z_J$ and variables numbered $J+1,\ldots,K$ are excluded. The equation would then appear as follows:

$$\beta_{g1}y_1 + \ldots + \beta_{gH}y_H + 0 + \ldots + 0 + \gamma_{g1}z_1 + \ldots + \gamma_{gJ}z_J + 0 + \ldots + 0 = 0$$

The first set of zeros correspond to the $G–H$ omitted endogenous variables and the second to the $K–J$ omitted predetermined variables.

The order condition said that the number of excluded variables should be at least as great as the number of equations less one. Given that we now have a specific expression for the number of excluded variables we can write the condition as

$$(G-H) + (K-J) \geqslant G-1.$$

The only reference to the size of the model in this inequality cancels out, and we can restate the order condition as

$$K-J \geqslant H-1$$

i.e. the number of predetermined variables in the model excluded from this equation must be not less than the number of included endogenous variables, less one. Hence we can assess identifiability without actually going ahead and spelling out the remainder of the model – we do not need to know how many equations it contains to check this identifiability condition, for our criterion no longer contains G. In practice therefore all we need do to apply the order condition to a structural equation is simply to count up the number of endogenous variables appearing in it (H) and argue that there are a certain number ($K-J$) of predetermined variables in the model but excluded from the equation by considering what the variables themselves might be. We do not necessarily have to specify the complete system in order to assess the identifiability of an individual equation. Nor do we need to know how many exogenous variables the total system contains so long as we have located enough of them to satisfy $K - J \geqslant H - 1$.

4.4 *The reduced form*

Now let us look at this from the point of view of estimating or identifying the parameter values of the structural equation from the reduced form. Equivalent order and rank conditions can be obtained in this framework. We shall see that calculation of the β and γ values from the reduced form is perfectly feasible if the equation is identified although we have already seen that, even in fairly simple cases, it can be a very cumbersome procedure. In practice one would therefore assess identifiability in precisely the way we have been doing it through the structural form.

The only relevant reduced form equations are going to be those for the included endogenous variables (i.e. the first H endogenous variables). The general reduced form equations include all K predetermined variables in the model though only J of them appear in our particular structural equation.

$$y_1 = \pi_{11}z_1 + \dots + \pi_{1J}z_J + \pi_{1,J+1}z_{J+1} + \dots + \pi_{1K}z_K \qquad (1)$$

$$y_2 = \pi_{21}z_1 + \dots + \pi_{2J}z_J + \pi_{2,J+1}z_{J+1} + \dots + \pi_{2K}z_K \qquad (2)$$

$$\vdots \qquad\qquad\qquad\qquad\qquad \vdots$$

$$y_H = \pi_{H1}z_1 + \dots + \pi_{HJ}z_J + \pi_{H,J+1}z_{J+1} + \dots + \pi_{HK}z_K \qquad (H)$$

Without loss of generality we can assume that the structural equation of interest is the first ($g=1$), and that we normalise on the first coefficient as usual. Thus the structural equation whose parameter values we require is

$$y_1 + \beta_{12}y_2 + \dots + \beta_{1H}y_H + \gamma_{11}z_1 + \dots + \gamma_{1J}z_J = 0.$$

The reduced form coefficient values are given by the data (they are identified), and if our structure equation satisfies the data, it must hold when values of $y_1,...,y_H$ are substituted from the reduced form. That is, when we take the right hand side of (1), plus β_{12} times the R.H.S. of (2), plus ... β_{1H} times the R.H.S. of (H), the resulting linear combination of the z's must exactly cancel out $\gamma_{11}z_1 + ... + \gamma_{1J}z_J$, so that our structure equation is satisfied. Note that the linear combination of reduced form equations involves all K z's: we require the first J of them to have a coefficient which will cancel with $\gamma_{11},...,\gamma_{1J}$, and the remaining K–J to have zero coefficients, as specified. These requirements are as follows:

$$\left.\begin{array}{llr} (z_1): & \pi_{11} + \beta_{12}\pi_{21} + ... + \beta_{1H}\pi_{H1} + \gamma_{11} & = 0 \\ \vdots & \vdots & \vdots \\ (z_J): & \pi_{1J} + \beta_{12}\pi_{2J} + ... + \beta_{1H}\pi_{HJ} + \gamma_{1J} & = 0 \end{array}\right\} J$$

$$\left.\begin{array}{llr} (z_{J+1}): & \pi_{1,J+1} + \beta_{12}\pi_{2,J+1} + ... + \beta_{1H}\pi_{H,J+1} & = 0 \\ \vdots & \vdots & \vdots \\ (z_K): & \pi_{1K} + \beta_{12}\pi_{2K} + ... + \beta_{1H}\pi_{HK} & = 0 \end{array}\right\} K-J$$

(If you are happier with the matrix formulation what we have here is the first row of the matrix equation $\mathbf{B\Pi} + \mathbf{\Gamma} = \mathbf{0}$.) Given numerical values of the π's, can these equations be solved for the β and γ values? There is no difficulty in solving the first J equations for the γ's provided that the β's are known, for these equations give $\gamma_{11},...,\gamma_{1J}$ in terms of β's and π's. But can we solve for the β-values? That question is resolved by the second block of K–J equations. The number of equations is K–J and the number of unknown β's is $H-1$. Immediately we have a reappearance of the order condition. A solution for the β's is only possible if the number of equations (K–J) is at least as great as the number of unknowns ($H-1$) i.e. $K-J \geqslant H-1$, and this condition is necessary. It is not sufficient because, if it is just satisfied ($K-J = H-1$) but the determinant of the coefficients of the unknown β's is zero, then we have a singular set of equations which cannot be solved. So we have an equivalent rank condition, that the rank of the matrix of coefficients in the K–J equations for the $H-1$ unknown β's be $H-1$. That is, we require the rank of the $(K-J)\times(H-1)$ matrix

$$\begin{bmatrix} \pi_{2,J+1} & \cdots & \pi_{H,J+1} \\ \vdots & & \vdots \\ \pi_{2K} & \cdots & \pi_{HK} \end{bmatrix}$$

to be $H-1$. This is again the necessary and sufficient condition – the rank of the matrix cannot be $H-1$ unless it also has at least $H-1$ rows, so the order condition is automatically satisfied whenever the rank condition is satisfied. When this is the case the second block of equations is solved for the values of $\beta_{12},...,\beta_{1H}$, and the values of $\gamma_{11},...,\gamma_{1J}$ immediately follow from the first block of equations.

So we have derived precisely equivalent identifiability conditions. In practice, this approach is rather more difficult because, to assess the rank condition in this framework, we need to obtain the reduced form. The rank condition as formulated earlier (p.57) does not require this exercise – we need only to look at particular matrices of structural coefficients to assess identifiability, which is somewhat easier. The two methods are, of course, equivalent.

4.5 *Identification by homogeneous linear restrictions on the coefficients*

Up to this point we have discussed identifiability in terms of excluding variables from an equation by assigning the value zero to particular parameters in the system. Though zero restrictions are common ways of incorporating theoretical information, they are merely special cases of homogeneous linear restrictions, and the order condition is easily extended to cover this more general restriction. For the general equation

$$\sum_i \beta_{gi} y_i + \sum_k \gamma_{gk} z_k = 0$$

the general homogeneous linear restriction is

$$\sum_{i=1}^{G} \lambda_i \beta_{gi} + \sum_{k=1}^{K} \theta_k \gamma_{gk} = 0$$

where the λ's and θ's are specified a priori. Thus $\beta_{g2} = 0$ (excluding y_2 from the gth equation) is the simplest example. If we specify that y_2 and y_3 appear with the same coefficient in the first equation, we have the restriction $\beta_{12}-\beta_{13} = 0$. Similarly, if they appear with equal and opposite coefficients we have $\beta_{12}+\beta_{13} = 0$ (recall the example presented on p.11). Note that if three variables, say z_1, z_2, and z_3, are all to appear with the same coefficient, we have two restrictions, say $\gamma_{11}-\gamma_{12} = 0$ and $\gamma_{11}-\gamma_{13} = 0$: the third restriction $\gamma_{12}-\gamma_{13} = 0$ is not required, it is not independent of the other two, being implied by them. One point about a homogeneous linear restriction is that it does not have a constant term in it: it equates to zero a linear combination of actual parameter values. However that does not provide any difficulty because no normalisation rule has yet been applied above. If we wanted to have some constant in the restriction on the first equation's coefficients rather than a zero on the right hand side, we could utilise the coefficient β_{11} being set equal to one in the normalisation rule. So if we wanted to impose constant returns to scale, for example, by specifying that the coefficients of y_2 and y_3 sum to one, we would write the restriction $\beta_{12}+\beta_{13}-\beta_{11}=0$ and incorporate the normalisation rule $\beta_{11}=1$.

The order condition for identifiability can be rewritten for this more general framework as follows:

In a G equation linear model a necessary condition for the identification of a single equation is that there are at least G–1 independent homogeneous linear restrictions on the parameters of the equation.

This order condition is slightly more general, for it contains the previous one as the special case in which the restrictions considered are all zero restrictions.

This order condition is frequently required when identities have been substituted into an equation system. For this typically introduces homogeneous linear restrictions into the other equations on eliminating a particular variable. In our earlier example, the assumption that consumption depends on disposable income could be written in terms of the following two equations, the first being a behavioural equation and the second an identity:

$$\begin{aligned} c &= \alpha + \beta y_d \\ y_d &= y - t \end{aligned} \qquad (1)$$

To assess the identifiability of a system including these equations we can either leave them as they stand (the identity is fully specified a priori and raises no question of identifiability) or simply substitute out y_d to give

$$c = \alpha + \beta(y - t) \qquad (2)$$

(This reduces the total number of equations, by one.) In this case there is a restriction on the parameters, since we are specifying that y and t appear in the consumption function with equal and opposite coefficients. That is, the sum of their coefficients is zero, and this restriction must be counted in assessing the identifiability of the consumption function. One would not expect that this substitution alters the conclusion about identifiability of the consumption function, for the basic system is the same. Suppose that there are n other variables (investment, interest rate, etc) appearing in the model, and that there are G equations before substitution – i.e. the equations (1), and G–2 others. Then the consumption function excludes all the n other variables and y and t, and is identified (by the order condition) if $n + 2 \geqslant G-1$. After substitution there are only $G-1$ equations. The equation (2) excludes the n other variables, and has one further homogeneous linear restriction, and is identified if $n+1 \geqslant G-2$, so the conclusion is the same either way. (cf. Exercise 4.2)

There is an analogous rank condition, but it will not be treated here*. However, in situations where homogeneous linear restrictions result from substituting out identities, we would expect it to give the same answer as the previous rank condition applied to the model containing the identities, because as noted in the preceding paragraph, nothing in the basic system is changed by this operation. And again, one would go ahead with estimation on the assumption that the particular function of parameters featuring in the rank condition is not zero.

Exercises

4.1 Consider the identification of each equation in the following model:

$$
\begin{aligned}
p_t + \beta_{12} w_t + \quad\quad + \gamma_{11} Q_t \quad\quad + \gamma_{13} p_{t-1} \quad\quad &= u_{1t} \\
\beta_{21} p_t + \quad w_t + \beta_{23} N_t \quad\quad + \gamma_{22} S_t \quad\quad + \gamma_{24} w_{t-1} &= u_{2t} \\
\beta_{32} w_t + \quad N_t \quad\quad + \gamma_{32} S_t + \gamma_{33} p_{t-1} + \gamma_{34} w_{t-1} &= u_{3t}
\end{aligned}
$$

where p_t, w_t and N_t are indices for prices, money wages and trade union membership (endogenous) and Q_t and S_t are indices for productivity and strikes (exogenous).
How are the rank and order conditions affected if it is known a priori that

(i) $\gamma_{11} = 0$
(ii) $\beta_{21} = \gamma_{22} = 0$
(iii) $\gamma_{33} = 0$

Comment on the statement that '. . . we shall be content with the fact that the rank condition is satisfied in nearly every case when the order condition is'.

*This is discussed in Ch.2 of F. M. Fisher, *The Identification Problem in Econometrics,* which is a more advanced treatment of the whole topic.

4.2 (*a*) Investigate the identifiability of the equations of the following model of two interrelated markets.

$$
\begin{array}{lllllll}
\text{(1) demand for first good:} & q_1 & +\beta_{11}p_1 & & +\beta_{13}p_3+\gamma_{10}+\gamma_{11}y & & = u_1 \\
\text{(2) supply of first good:} & q_1 & +\beta_{21}p_1 & & +\gamma_{20} & & = u_2 \\
\text{(3) demand for second good:} & q_2 & +\beta_{31}p_1 & & +\beta_{33}p_3+\gamma_{30}+\gamma_{31}y & +\gamma_{32}w & = u_3 \\
\text{(4) supply of second good:} & q_2 & & +\beta_{42}p_2 & +\gamma_{40} & +\gamma_{42}w & = u_4 \\
\text{(5) excise tax:} & & & p_2 & -p_3 & +E & = 0
\end{array}
$$

endogenous variables: q_1,q_2,p_1,p_2,p_3; exogenous variables: y,w,E. p_2 is the price of the second good before tax, p_3 the price of the second good after tax.

(*b*) Consider the following model, equivalent to that given above.

$$
\begin{array}{lllllll}
(1) & q_1 & +\beta_{11}p_1+\beta_{13}p_2+\gamma_{10}+\gamma_{11}y & & & +\beta_{13}E & = u_1 \\
(2) & q_1 & +\beta_{21}p_1 & +\gamma_{20} & & & = u_2 \\
(3) & q_2 & +\beta_{31}p_1+\beta_{33}p_2+\gamma_{30}+\gamma_{31}y & & +\gamma_{32}w & +\beta_{33}E & = u_3 \\
(4) & q_2 & +\beta_{42}p_2 & +\gamma_{40} & +\gamma_{42}w & & = u_4
\end{array}
$$

Evaluate any similarities or differences between the identifiability of the parameters of this model and that of part (a).

Chapter 5

ESTIMATION

5.1 *Introduction*

We now consider estimation of the parameters of our general linear model in either its structural form $\mathbf{B}\mathbf{y}_t + \Gamma\mathbf{z}_t = \mathbf{u}_t$ or its reduced form $\mathbf{y}_t = \Pi\mathbf{z}_t + \mathbf{v}_t$ given a sample of data $\mathbf{y}_t, \mathbf{z}_t, t = 1,...,T$. In general this data may be either time series or cross section data, but time series data is more common. The appropriate estimation technique and the properties of the estimators vary according to a number of features of the problem at hand.

First, they depend upon assumptions about the random error terms in the model, where we can distinguish three stages:
(a) we usually assume that the errors have zero means and constant variances, also that the covariances between the errors in different equations are constant over time.
(b) we may in addition require the absence of autocorrelation, and assume that the succeeding values of a given error term over time are independent.
(c) when discussing statistical hypothesis testing procedures we may also assume that the errors are normally distributed.

Secondly, we shall find that the situation varies with the assumptions we make about the predetermined variables. The simplest cases are obtained when they are assumed to be entirely exogenous but we shall also consider the consequences for estimation of assuming some elements of $\mathbf{z}_t$ to be lagged endogenous variables.

Thirdly, we may distinguish between methods which are appropriate for estimating reduced form equations and those applicable to structural equations. It turns out that reduced form estimation is in general easier and we shall first consider ordinary least squares (OLS) estimation of a reduced form equation. We shall then show that when OLS is applied to a structural equation all sorts of problems arise and the conventional results no longer apply, except in very special circumstances. We shall consider structural equation estimation by means of indirect least squares, instrumental variables, and two stage least squares methods.

Finally, we may distinguish methods which can cope with a single equation at a time from those which are designed for estimating the complete model in one go. Methods designed for estimating an entire structure subject to all the identifying restrictions in the model simultaneously, such as three stage least squares or full information maximum likelihood, will not be discussed. We shall confine ourselves to the techniques mentioned above.

5.2 *OLS estimation of a reduced form equation; simple regression.*

We begin by considering least squares estimation of a reduced form equation, thus the only endogenous variable in the equation is the dependent variable, and all the explanatory variables are predetermined. The standard case is one in which all predetermined variables are exogenous, this being necessary for some of the properties of OLS estimates to hold.

The typical reduced form equation is

$$y_{it} = \sum_{k=1}^{K} \pi_{ik} z_{kt} + v_{it}$$

and as it makes no difference which one of the G equations is being estimated, we shall drop the i subscripts for the time being. We first consider the simplest case, where the equation to be estimated contains only one exogenous variable, (also avoiding matrix algebra) so we can drop the k subscript as well. The intercept term is denoted by α, so the equation to be estimated is

$$y_t = \alpha + \pi z_t + v_t, \qquad t = 1, ..., T.$$

The basic model is that the observations y_t are generated by superimposing the random error or disturbance, v_t, on the systematic, linear, part of the relationship. The statistician may often have in mind the situation where the z_t values can be regarded as a set of constants, chosen and kept fixed while an experiment is repeated a number of times, each replication giving rise to different y–values due to the random variation in v. In non-experimental sciences, the z_t values are given to us, and we seldom have repeated observations on y for a given z–value, nevertheless our exogeneity assumptions often enable us to get to the same results. The model is often represented by sketching the probability distribution of the superimposed error at each z–value; a given sample of observations $y_1,...,y_T$ results from taking a sample of one error term from each distribution.

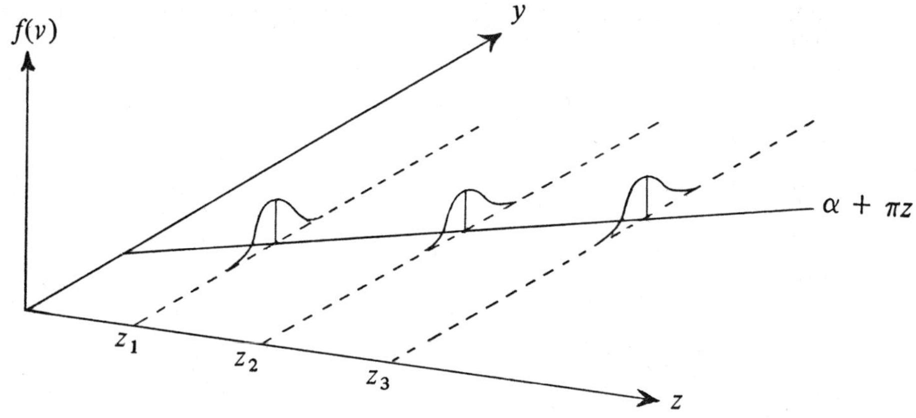

From these observations we attempt to disentangle the systematic part of the relationship by calculating estimates a and p of the parameters α and π, giving the estimated regression line

$$\hat{y}_t = a + pz_t.$$

(We use the corresponding roman letter to denote an estimate of a parameter represented by a greek letter; hats denote regression estimates of variables.) The discrepancies between the observations y_t and the estimated values $\hat{y}_t$ are referred to as regression *residuals:*

$$\hat{\nu}_t = y_t - \hat{y}_t = y_t - a - pz_t, \qquad t = 1,\ldots,T$$

which can be regarded as estimates of the unobservable errors, ν_t.

We adopt the *least squares* method of estimation, and choose for a given set of data those estimates a and p which minimise the sum of the squared residuals,

$$S = \sum_{t=1}^{T} \hat{\nu}_t^2 = \sum_{t=1}^{T} (y_t - \hat{y}_t)^2 = \sum_{t=1}^{T} (y_t - a - pz_t)^2.$$

S is minimised with respect to a and p by setting the first partial derivatives equal to zero, and remembering that the derivative of a sum is the sum of the derivatives of each term taken separately, this gives

$$\frac{\partial S}{\partial a} = \sum_{t=1}^{T} 2(y_t - a - pz_t)(-1) = 0$$

$$\frac{\partial S}{\partial p} = \sum_{t=1}^{T} 2(y_t - a - pz_t)(-z_t) = 0.$$

Upon rearrangement we have the so-called *normal equations of least squares:*

$$\Sigma y_t = Ta + p\Sigma z_t$$
$$\Sigma y_t z_t = a\Sigma z_t + p\Sigma z_t^2.$$

Solving these equations for a and p we have by dividing the first equation by T

$$\bar{y} = a + p\bar{z}$$

where $\bar{y}$ and $\bar{z}$ are the respective sample means, hence

$$a = \bar{y} - p\bar{z}.$$

Substituting into the second equation gives

$$\begin{aligned}\Sigma y_t z_t &= p\Sigma z_t^2 + (\bar{y} - p\bar{z})\,\Sigma z_t \\ &= p\Sigma z_t^2 + (\bar{y} - p\bar{z})\,T\bar{z},\end{aligned}$$

therefore

$$p = \frac{\Sigma y_t z_t - T\bar{y}\bar{z}}{\Sigma z_t^2 - T\bar{z}^2} = \frac{\Sigma(y_t - \bar{y})(z_t - \bar{z})}{\Sigma(z_t - \bar{z})^2}.$$

So we first calculate p according to this expression, and then calculate a as $\bar{y} - p\bar{z}$. Computer programs typically go on to print out for $t = 1,\ldots,T$ the observed values (y_t), the predicted values $(a+pz_t)$, and the difference between them $(\hat{v}_t)$ – the residuals corresponding to minimum S. Note that the residuals sum to zero, for

$$\begin{aligned}\sum_{t=1}^{T} \hat{v}_t &= \Sigma(y_t - a - pz_t) \\ &= \Sigma y_t - Ta - p\Sigma z_t \\ &= T\bar{y} - T(\bar{y} - p\bar{z}) - pT\bar{z} = 0.\end{aligned}$$

From this fact it is clear that, if we look at the regression residuals to see if they contain any systematic influence which should be accounted for in some way, we should not expect to identify any such factor in terms of the residuals' mean. Although the sample mean of the residuals is zero, this will not in general be true of the errors v_t.

Sums of squares and cross-products around sample means will crop up fairly often in what follows, and an abbreviated notation is sometimes convenient. Such expressions are known as moments (or, more fully, sample second moments about the mean) and are denoted by the letter m with two subscripts. Thus

$$m_{yz} = \sum_{t=1}^{T} (y_t - \bar{y})(z_t - \bar{z}), \qquad m_{zz} = \sum_{t=1}^{T} (z_t - \bar{z})^2,$$

and $p = m_{yz}/m_{zz}$.

Note that in calculating a quantity such as m_{yz} we only need to correct one of the variables for the mean and not both of them. That is,

$$\begin{aligned} m_{yz} = \Sigma(y_t - \bar{y})(z_t - \bar{z}) &= \Sigma y_t(z_t - \bar{z}) - \bar{y}\,\Sigma(z_t - \bar{z}) \\ &= \Sigma y_t(z_t - \bar{z}), \end{aligned}$$

since $\bar{y}$ is constant as t varies and so is brought outside the summation, and $(z_t - \bar{z})$ sums to zero over t by definition of the sample mean $\bar{z}$.

Properties of least squares estimates

So far we have made no assumptions about v, and we can carry out the least squares calculations without making assumptions about the underlying situation. However the method will only have optimal properties under certain assumptions. Let us begin by assuming that

$$E(v_t) = 0, \text{ and } E(v_t^2) = \omega^2 \text{ for all } t \text{ (i.e. variance constant over time)}$$

We have already seen that the sample mean of the residuals is zero. Can we find an estimator for ω^2? It is natural to seek one from the minimised residual sum of squares. (The residuals already are in mean deviation form, i.e. $\Sigma(\hat{v}_t - \bar{\hat{v}})^2 = \Sigma\, \hat{v}_t^2$). It turns out that to get an unbiased estimate of the variance one should in general divide $\Sigma\, \hat{v}_t^2$ by T–K, where K is the number of estimated coefficients. Hence an unbiased estimate of ω^2 is given for our simple case by

$$w^2 = \frac{1}{T-2} \; \Sigma \hat{v}_t^2$$

The first consideration about the least squares estimates is whether the coefficients a and p are *unbiased* estimates of α and π. Let us consider p in particular and, within the hypothetical framework of repeated sampling, ask: if we fix the values $z_1, \ldots, z_T$, then observe the y's and calculate the coefficient p which results from a given sample of v's, and do this many times for the same z's, in the long run is the average value of p equal to π ($E(p) = \pi$)? It is clear that we do need some assumptions about the error term to answer this question, for the statistical properties of p depend on those of v.

It is convenient to work in mean deviation form. By taking the original equation

$$y_t = \alpha + \pi z_t + v_t,$$

summing over T observations and dividing by T, we have

$$\bar{y} = \alpha + \pi \bar{z} + \bar{v}$$

which on subtracting gives

$$y_t - \bar{y} = \pi(z_t - \bar{z}) + (v_t - \bar{v}).$$

(NB. $\bar{v}$ is the sample mean of the errors and must be distinguished from the theoretical mean $E(v)$.)

Now we express p in terms of v in order to study its statistical properties, by substituting from this last equation.

$$p = \frac{\Sigma(y_t - \bar{y})(z_t - \bar{z})}{(z_t - \bar{z})^2} = \frac{\Sigma[\pi(z_t - \bar{z}) + (v_t - \bar{v})](z_t - \bar{z})}{\Sigma(z_t - \bar{z})^2}$$

Multiplying out the terms in the square brackets and simplifying:

$$p = \pi + \frac{\Sigma(v_t - \bar{v})(z_t - \bar{z})}{\Sigma(z_t - \bar{z})^2} = \pi + \Sigma(v_t - \bar{v}) \left\{ \frac{z_t - \bar{z}}{\Sigma(z_t - \bar{z})^2} \right\}.$$

Now we are in a position to see whether $E(p) = \pi$. We recall that the expected value of a sum of terms is equal to the sum of the expected values of each term considered separately, and so

$$E(p) = \pi + \Sigma E \left[(v_t - \bar{v}) \left\{ \frac{z_t - \bar{z}}{\Sigma(z_t - \bar{z})^2} \right\} \right]$$

Now if the z-values are fixed numbers the next step is easy, for the expected value of a constant multiplied by a random variable is equal to the constant multiplied by the expected value of the random variable, and so

$$E(p) = \pi + \Sigma \left\{ \frac{z_t - \bar{z}}{\Sigma(z_t - \bar{z})^2} \right\} E(v_t - \bar{v})$$

But $E(v_t) = 0$, and so $E(\bar{v}) = 0$, hence every element in the summation is zero, and $E(p) = \pi$.

If the z is a random variable itself, but exogenous and so independent of v, we need one extra step. Independence of two random variables implies that the expected value of their product is equal to the product of their separate expected values, and so

$$E(p) = \pi + \Sigma E(v_t - \bar{v}) E \left\{ \frac{z_t - \bar{z}}{\Sigma(z_t - \bar{z})^2} \right\}$$

Again $E(v_t) = E(\bar{v}) = 0$, hence $E(p) = \pi$, and p is an *unbiased* estimate of π. In any single sample p will not equal π, there will be a sampling error $p-\pi$, but these will average out to zero in repeated samples.

Notice that no assumption has been made about the presence or absence of autocorrelation in the v_t series, nor have we used the assumption about the variance of v_t being constant – p is unbiased either way. Trouble arises, however, when z_t is a lagged endogenous variable, for $E\left[(v_t-v)\left\{\frac{z_t-\bar{z}}{\Sigma(z_t-\bar{z})^2}\right\}\right]$ can no longer be split into a product of two expected values as the two factors inside the square brackets are not independent. For a lagged endogenous variable to be predetermined we require its independence of current and future disturbances, but we cannot require independence of past errors. (If z_t is the lagged dependent variable, $z_t = y_{t-1}$, then z_t depends on v_{t-1}.) So v_t in the first factor is related to some z_{t+j} which appears in the denominator of the second factor, and independence no longer holds, and we cannot prove $E(p) = \pi$ – in general there will be a bias $E(p) - \pi \neq 0$. To summarise:

Is $E(p) = \pi$?

z_t \ v_t	*serially independent*	*autocorrelated*
exogenous	Yes	Yes
lagged endogenous	No	No

(Note that the unbiasedness proof also breaks down if the explanatory variable is any endogenous variable, lagged or not. This arises when we estimate a structural equation rather than a reduced form equation, and we shall consider this later.)

One might be tempted to try and prove unbiasedness in the lagged endogenous case by working with

$$E(p) = \pi + E\frac{\Sigma(v_t-\bar{v})(z_t-\bar{z})}{\Sigma(z_t-\bar{z})^2}$$

and (ignoring $\bar{v}$ and $\bar{z}$) arguing that v_t and z_t only appear contemporaneously in the numerator, and $E(v_t z_t) = 0$ even in this case. This is no help, for it is not in general true that the expected value of a ratio of two variables is equal to the ratio of the expected values of numerator and denominator taken separately,

i.e. $E\left[\frac{x_1}{x_2}\right] \neq \frac{E(x_1)}{E(x_2)}$. So it is no use arguing about the numerator alone.

This explains why the last term in the above equation was rearranged in the earlier discussion.

Variance of p. An unbiased estimator which has a large variance around the true parameter value will be of less use than one which has a small variance; in repeated sampling, we would like to keep the sampling errors $p-\pi$ as small as possible, and an index of their variation is provided by the variance of p,

$$\begin{aligned} \text{var}(p) &= E[p-E(p)]^2 \\ &= E(p-\pi)^2 \qquad \text{if } p \text{ is unbiased.} \end{aligned}$$

The following derivation either assumes that the z variable is a set of fixed constants (e.g. a trend variable), or obtains var(p) conditional upon the actual observed values of z_t if this is assumed to be exogenous. We also require v_t to be non-autocorrelated, i.e. $E(v_t v_s) = 0$ for $t \neq s$.

From an equation on p.72 we have

$$p = \pi + \frac{\Sigma v_t(z_t-\bar{z})}{\Sigma(z_t-\bar{z})^2},$$

and so

$$\text{var}(p) = E(p-\pi)^2 = E\left\{\sum_{t=1}^{T} v_t \frac{(z_t-\bar{z})}{\sum_j (z_j-\bar{z})^2}\right\}^2$$

On squaring the above summation two kinds of terms appear. On the one hand we have the squares of the elements in the sum, involving terms like v_t^2, and on the other hand a host of cross-products, involving terms like $v_t v_s$. Here all the cross products have a zero expected value precisely because of the assumption that the v's are serially independent, and we have:

$$\begin{aligned} E(p-\pi)^2 &= E\sum_{t=1}^{T}\left\{v_t \frac{(z_t-\bar{z})}{\sum_j (z_j-\bar{z})^2}\right\}^2 \\ &= \sum_{t=1}^{T} Ev_t^2 \frac{(z_t-\bar{z})^2}{[\sum_j (z_j-z)^2]^2} \end{aligned}$$

Since $E(v_t^2) = \text{var}(v) = \omega^2$ for all t, and either the z-values are constants or we are deriving var(p) conditionally upon the observed values of an exogenous z, we have

$$\text{var}(p) = \frac{\omega^2}{\Sigma(z_t - \bar{z})^2}.$$

Notice that the bigger the variance of the error term the larger the variance of the estimated slope coefficient: i.e. the more random variation there is around the regression line the more variable will be our estimate of the regression coefficient. Also the denominator increases and so var(p) decreases as the sample size T increases. It is possible to show that this variance is the smallest that can be attained by any linear unbiased estimator, under these assumptions, whereupon it is often stated that the least squares estimator is the best linear unbiased estimator.

We have now discussed the two main properties of the sample statistic p – the mean and the variance. Suppose now that our assumptions are such that we cannot prove unbiasedness, can we say anything further? Can we make useful statements about the case where the z's are lagged endogenous?

Asymptotic properties: consistency. In a number of situations it is only possible to derive properties of estimators as the sample size T tends to infinity. If no results concerning bias, variance and so forth are obtainable for finite samples, then the limiting case is the best we can do. The asymptotic property we shall consider is that of *consistency.* p is a consistent estimator of π if the sampling distribution of p approaches a degenerate distribution with all the probability concentrated at the value π as the sample size T becomes infinite. We then say the probability limit of p is π, and write

$$\underset{T\to\infty}{\text{plim}}\, p = \pi$$

Let us consider the possibility of repeating our regression experiment for a given set of z values by drawing a number of samples of T errors, $v_1,\dots,v_T$, (T fixed) and calculating p for each sample of y values that results. If we do this sufficiently often we shall obtain a smooth distribution of p values – the mean and variance of this sampling distribution have already been found for some cases. Now repeat the whole process for a new, larger value of T, the sample size, and obtain another distribution of p values. Consistency requires that as we do this for larger and larger sample sizes, the resulting distribution of p collapses at the true value π, which we can illustrate as follows.

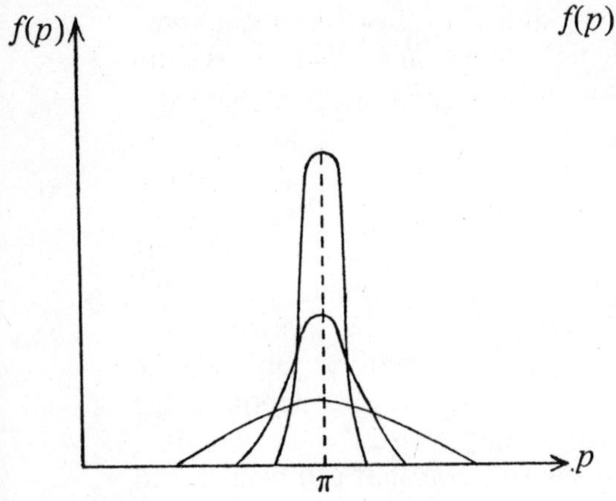

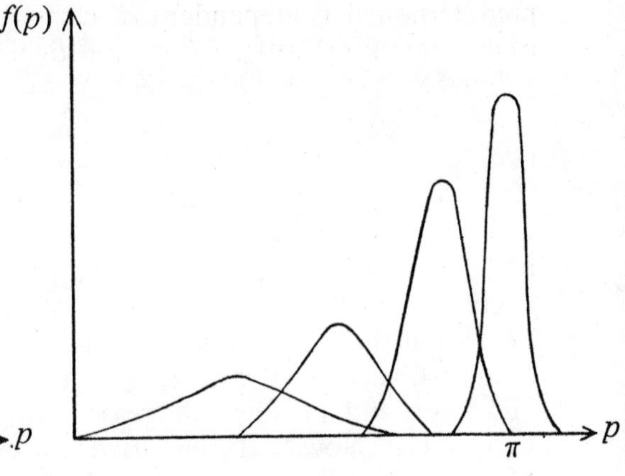

The second diagram illustrates a situation in which the estimate is biased in small (finite) samples, and so for it to be consistent two things must happen as T increases – the distribution must move over and centre itself at π, as well as becoming narrower and narrower as in the first diagram.

This heuristic discussion has rested upon two conditions which are actually sufficient conditions for consistency – asymptotic unbiasedness and a variance going to zero. Typically this is how one would prove consistency; i.e. if $\lim_{T\to\infty} E(p) = \pi$ and $\lim_{T\to\infty} \text{var}(p) = 0$, then $\text{plim}\,(p) = \pi$. In the simplest case of exogenous z and independent v's, p is a consistent estimate of π because, as we have shown, $E(p) = \pi$ for all sample sizes (not just large ones) and $\text{var}(p) = \omega^2/\Sigma(z_t-\bar{z})^2 \to 0$ as $T \to \infty$ since the sum $\Sigma(z_t-\bar{z})^2$ increases indefinitely as the number of (positive) terms increases.

Plims have a very useful property that enables us to overcome the difficulty found on p.74: the plim of a function of two random variables is equal to the value of the function when the separate plims of the two variables are substituted in, and specifically $\text{plim}\,\dfrac{x_1}{x_2} = \dfrac{\text{plim}(x_1)}{\text{plim}(x_2)}$ (assuming that $\text{plim}(x_2)$ exists and is non-zero). The previous difficulty with the lagged endogenous case can now be overcome, for we also have

$$\lim_{T\to\infty} E\left[\Sigma v_t \, \frac{(z_t-\bar{z})}{\Sigma(z_t-\bar{z})^2}\right] = \frac{\lim E\,\frac{1}{T}\,\Sigma v_t(z_t-\bar{z})}{\text{plim}\,\frac{1}{T}\,\Sigma(z_t-\bar{z})^2}$$

enabling us to consider the question of bias in large samples. (We divide top and bottom by T to ensure that the denominator remains finite as $T \to \infty$ – it is now the variance of z.) Now if z is predetermined (independent of current and future disturbances) we obtain a numerator of zero, giving the result that p is an asymptotically unbiased estimate of π. It is also possible to go on to prove consistency. However even these devices do not help if z is lagged endogenous and v is autocorrelated – we showed previously (p. 41) that in this case there is a non-zero covariance between z_t and v_t, which does not go away as T increases. So the eventual conclusions are:

Is p a consistent estimator of π, i.e. plim $p = \pi$?

z_t \ v_t	*serially independent*	*autocorrelated*
exogenous	Yes	Yes
lagged endogenous	Yes	No

The only change from the finite sample bias results (p. 73) is in the bottom left hand corner – here the bias goes to zero as T increases.

Goodness of fit

Now we leave the theoretical properties of our estimates and return to our regression line, asking how well does it fit the observations? We can regard the observed values y_t as being split up into two parts – the regression estimate $\hat{y}_t$ and the residual $\hat{v}_t$. From the definition of the regression residual, we have

$$y_t = \hat{y}_t + \hat{v}_t \qquad t = 1,\ldots,T$$

We showed that the residuals have a zero mean, and so the observed values and regression estimates of y have equal means, i.e. $\bar{y} = \bar{\hat{y}}$. (Since $\bar{y} = a + p\bar{z}$, the regression line passes through the point $(\bar{y}, \bar{z})$ – the sample means of the original variables. This point also corresponds to the sample mean of the regression estimate.) The sum of squared deviations from the mean of the y series can be similarly split up into two parts -- a part due to the regression estimates and a part due to the residuals. We have

$$\sum_{t=1}^{T} (y_t - \bar{y})^2 = \Sigma(\hat{y}_t - \bar{y} + \hat{v}_t)^2$$
$$= \Sigma(\hat{y}_t - \bar{y})^2 + \Sigma\hat{v}_t^2 + 2\,\Sigma\hat{v}_t(\hat{y}_t - \bar{y}),$$

and we now show that the last term is zero. We have

$$\hat{y}_t - \bar{y} = a + pz_t - \bar{y} = p(z_t - \bar{z}), \text{ since } a = \bar{y} - p\bar{z},$$

and $$\hat{v}_t = y_t - \hat{y}_t = y_t - \bar{y} - p(z_t - \bar{z}),$$

thus $$\Sigma\hat{v}_t(\hat{y}_t - \bar{y}) = p\Sigma(z_t - \bar{z})(y_t - \bar{y}) - p^2\Sigma(z_t - \bar{z})^2,$$

which is zero since $p = \dfrac{\Sigma(z_t - \bar{z})(y_t - \bar{y})}{\Sigma(z_t - \bar{z})^2}$.

To repeat the conclusion: the sum of squares of the original observations around their mean (the 'original sum of squares') can be exactly partitioned into the explained sum of squares (or 'sum of squares due to regression') $\Sigma(\hat{y}_t - \bar{y})^2$, plus the residual or unexplained sum of squares, $\Sigma\hat{v}_t^2$. We can replace the phrase 'sum of squares' everywhere in this sentence by the word 'variance' if we divide the equation through by T. The regression estimates and the residuals have zero covariance.

However the explained sum of squares does not provide a useful index of how well the regression line fits the data unless it is related to the original sum of squares. A standardised measure of goodness of fit is provided by the coefficient of determination, or multiple correlation coefficient, R^2, which can be defined as

$$R^2 = \frac{\textit{explained sum of squares}}{\textit{original sum of squares}}$$

$$= \frac{\Sigma(\hat{y}_t - \bar{y})^2}{\Sigma(y_t - \bar{y})^2} = 1 - \frac{\Sigma\hat{v}_t^2}{\Sigma(y_t - \bar{y})^2}, \quad 0 \leq R^2 \leq 1.$$

Note that in computing the explained or residual sum of squares it is not necessary to calculate every regression estimate $\hat{y}_t$, $t = 1,\ldots,T$, since from the derivation in the previous paragraph $\Sigma(\hat{y}_t - \bar{y})^2 = p^2\Sigma(z_t - \bar{z})^2 = p\Sigma(z_t - \bar{z})(y_t - \bar{y})$. You might check that in the simple regression case, R^2 is the square of the ordinary coefficient of correlation between y and z,

$$\text{i.e. } R^2 = \left[\frac{\Sigma(z_t - \bar{z})(y_t - \bar{y})}{\sqrt{\Sigma(z_t - \bar{z})^2\,\Sigma(y_t - \bar{y})^2}}\right]^2$$

Significance of coefficients.

Apart from testing whether the regression as a whole explains the dependent variable satisfactorily, we can also test individual regression coefficients. We might wish to determine whether a particular calculated value of p is consistent with the hypothesis that π is some given number. Typically one examines individual coefficients to assess whether they are significantly different from zero, that is, one tests the hypothesis $\pi = 0$. The expression that we have already derived for var(p) effectively defines for us the nature of the sampling variation that we are likely to find around the true value of the parameter we are trying to estimate. We therefore encounter the familiar statistical problem of assessing an estimate against its sampling variability.

We know that the sampling error $p - \pi$ has expected value of zero and variance $\omega^2/\Sigma(z_t - \bar{z})^2$, and $p - \pi = \dfrac{\Sigma(z_t - \bar{z})v_t}{\Sigma(z_t - \bar{z})^2}$ so that if $v_1,\ldots,v_T$ have a normal distribution, then so does $p - \pi$. However there is a slight problem which has to be overcome before we can use this statement for hypothesis testing – var(p) is not known, since ω^2, the variance of v, is not known. But ω^2 is estimated by w^2, the residual sum of squares divided by the degrees of freedom (T–K in general, T–2 in this case), and so var(p) can be estimated as $w^2/\Sigma(z_t - \bar{z})^2$. It is customary to refer to the estimated standard deviation of the sampling distribution of a coefficient as its standard error, and so the standard error of p is

$$S.E.(p) = \frac{w^2}{\Sigma(z_t - z)^2} = \frac{\Sigma\hat{v}_t^2/(T-2)}{\Sigma(z_t - \bar{z})^2}$$

(Note that w is sometimes referred to as the 'standard error of the regression' or the 'standard error of estimate'.)

Under the assumption that the error term is normally distributed the ratio $t = \dfrac{p - \pi}{S.E.(p)}$ has a t distribution with T–2 degrees of freedom, and can be used to test hypotheses about π. The usual null hypothesis is that $\pi = 0$ but there may be cases where we want to test whether a coefficient is significantly different from some other number (say, $\pi = 1$). All we need do in any case is to follow the conventional hypothesis testing procedure, plug the hypothesised value of π into $\dfrac{p - \pi}{S.E.(p)}$ and compare it with the tabulated t distribution with T–2 degrees of freedom. If the result is a relatively small number we say that p is not so different from π as to cause us to reject the hypothesis, that is, we say that the observed difference between p and the hypothesised value of π is not significant, and probably arose due to sampling variability alone. If the result is a relatively large number we shall be unable to accept the hypothesised value of π, and we say that p is significantly different from that value – the discrepancy is too great to be attributed to sampling variability. For example, with the usual null hypothesis $H_0 : \pi = 0$ we calculate the t-ratio $\dfrac{p}{S.E.(p)}$ and compare this calculated value with the percentage points of the t distribution with $T-2$ degrees of freedom. If one is using a standard computer regression programme then the t-ratios are printed out together with the list of coefficient estimates (a and p in the bivariate reduced form case we have in mind) and their standard errors.

The use of the t distribution depends on the assumed normality of the distribution of the errors. If we wished to avoid making that assumption we would have to rely on an approximation which becomes valid as the sample size increases, namely that $(p-\pi)/S.E.(p)$ has a normal distribution. (This relies on the Central Limit Theorem; compare, for example, tests of significance of a sample mean.) Of course the t distribution itself approaches the normal distribution as T increases. The approximation is not too unreasonable for samples of 30 or more. In carrying out tests at the 5% significance level, the critical value of a normally distributed test statistic is 1.96. This has led to a simple rule of thumb being applied in testing the conventional null hypothesis that $\pi = 0$: a coefficient is said to be significantly different from zero if its absolute value is more than twice its standard error.

In reporting empirical work, it is the usual practice to present either standard errors or t-ratios (and it is important to be told which) in parentheses underneath the coefficient estimates. Note that in the bivariate, simple regression case we have been considering, R^2 and the t-ratio for p effectively measure the same thing – it is not possible to have a significant proportion of the original variance explained by the regression without a significant regression coefficient. However, in the multiple regression case to which we now turn, these questions are different – R^2 measures the fit of the regression as a whole, while t-ratios measure the effect of individual regression variables.

5.3 *Multiple regression*

We now consider a regression equation with more than one explanatory variable, but remain within reduced form estimation so that the only endogenous variable is the dependent variable:

$$y_t = \sum_{k=1}^{K} \pi_k z_{kt} + v_t, \qquad t = 1,...,T. \tag{1}$$

Again it doesn't matter which one of the G reduced form equations we are working with, so we continue to suppress the i subscripts. In terms of the general notation for linear models, we are concerned with the estimation of a single row of the $G \times K$ Π matrix, and we shall shortly see that it is more convenient for our present purposes to write the K coefficients in a *column* vector.

An intercept term can be incorporated in this formulation if required by defining one variable, say z_K, to be equal to one for all T observations, whereupon π_K becomes the constant term. However this could again be eliminated by working in mean deviations, when (1) can be written

$$y_t - \bar{y} = \sum_{k=1}^{K-1} \pi_k (z_{kt} - \bar{z}_k) + (v_t - \bar{v}), \qquad t = 1,\ldots,T.$$

This is of the same form as (1), if variables are defined as mean deviations, and since it makes little difference in what follows we shall adopt the first formulation, which is less clumsy, leaving the reader to define the variables either as mean deviations or as original observations according to taste.

Writing out the equation for each of the T observations we have the matrix representation

$$\begin{bmatrix} y_1 \\ y_2 \\ \cdot \\ \cdot \\ \cdot \\ y_T \end{bmatrix} = \begin{bmatrix} z_{11} & z_{21} & \cdots & z_{K1} \\ z_{12} & z_{22} & \cdots & z_{K2} \\ \cdot & \cdot & & \\ \cdot & \cdot & & \\ \cdot & \cdot & & \\ z_{1T} & z_{2T} & \cdots & z_{KT} \end{bmatrix} \begin{bmatrix} \pi_1 \\ \pi_2 \\ \cdot \\ \cdot \\ \cdot \\ \pi_K \end{bmatrix} + \begin{bmatrix} v_1 \\ v_2 \\ \cdot \\ \cdot \\ \cdot \\ v_T \end{bmatrix}$$

Defining $\mathbf{y}$, $\boldsymbol{\pi}$, and $\mathbf{v}$ as the above column vectors, and $\mathbf{Z}$ as the above matrix of observations on the predetermined variables, the equation can be written

$$\mathbf{y} = \mathbf{Z}\boldsymbol{\pi} + \mathbf{v}.$$

Notice that retaining our habitual ordering of subscripts whereby z_{kt} is the tth observation on the kth variable, but defining $\mathbf{Z}$ as the above TXK data matrix is at variance with the usual matrix algebra practice, where the first subscript denotes the row and the second the column of the matrix in which the element appears. (This definition of data matrices, with all the observations on a given variable forming a given column, is commonplace in econometrics – see, for example, the texts by Goldberger,[1] Johnston,[2] and Theil.[3] However, in Christ's text the matrix algebra convention is preserved by calling the above matrix $\mathbf{Z}'$, so his formulae are transpositions of everyone else's. Also Wonnacott and Wonnacott[4] preserve the convention by denoting the tth observation on the kth variable z_{tk}, which is equally unconventional.)

1. A. S. Goldberger, *Econometric Theory*, (Wiley).
2. J. Johnston, *Econometric Methods*, (McGraw-Hill).
3. H. Theil, *Principles of Econometrics*, (North-Holland).
4. R. J. and T. H. Wonnacott, *Econometrics*, (Wiley).

So $\mathbf{Z}$ is a $T \times K$ matrix with all T observations on the kth variable forming the kth column. If the variables are measured in original units, not in mean deviations, then $\mathbf{Z}$ will usually contain a column of ones to give an estimated intercept term. In accordance with previous notational conventions, $\mathbf{p} = (p_1, p_2, \ldots, p_K)'$ is a column vector of estimated coefficients, $\hat{\mathbf{y}} = \mathbf{Zp}$ is a column vector of regression estimates and $\hat{\mathbf{v}} = \mathbf{y} - \hat{\mathbf{y}}$ is a column vector of regression residuals, so $\hat{\mathbf{v}} = \mathbf{y} - \mathbf{Zp}$. We assume that $T > K$.

Least squares estimates

The following derivation of least squares estimates differs from those often found in that matrix differentiation is avoided. As before, we seek those estimates $(p_1, p_2, \ldots, p_K)$ which minimise the residual sum of squares $S = \sum_{t=1}^{T} \hat{v}_t^2$,

i.e. $$S = \Sigma \hat{v}_t^2 = \hat{\mathbf{v}}'\hat{\mathbf{v}} = (\mathbf{y} - \mathbf{Zp})'(\mathbf{y} - \mathbf{Zp}).$$

We shall seek a *linear* estimator, that is, an estimator which is a linear function of the observations on the dependent variable, so we write $\mathbf{p} = \mathbf{Cy}$ where $\mathbf{C}$ is a $K \times T$ matrix, and now we need to find that matrix $\mathbf{C}$ which minimises

$$S = (\mathbf{y}' - \mathbf{y}'\mathbf{C}'\mathbf{Z}')(\mathbf{y} - \mathbf{ZCy}).$$

Manipulating this expression, we have

$$S = \mathbf{y}'(\mathbf{I} - \mathbf{C}'\mathbf{Z}')(\mathbf{I} - \mathbf{ZC})\mathbf{y}$$ factoring out $\mathbf{y}$, where $\mathbf{I}$ is the $T \times T$ unit matrix

$$= \mathbf{y}'(\mathbf{I} - \mathbf{C}'\mathbf{Z}' - \mathbf{ZC} + \mathbf{C}'\mathbf{Z}'\mathbf{ZC})\mathbf{y}$$ multiplying out

$$= \mathbf{y}'[\mathbf{I} - \mathbf{Z}(\mathbf{Z}'\mathbf{Z})^{-1}\mathbf{Z}' + \mathbf{Z}(\mathbf{Z}'\mathbf{Z})^{-1}\mathbf{Z}' - \mathbf{C}'\mathbf{Z}' - \mathbf{ZC} + \mathbf{C}'\mathbf{Z}'\mathbf{ZC}]\mathbf{y}$$ adding and subtracting the same quantity

$$= \mathbf{y}'[\mathbf{I} - \mathbf{Z}(\mathbf{Z}'\mathbf{Z})^{-1}\mathbf{Z}']\mathbf{y} + \mathbf{y}'[\mathbf{Z}(\mathbf{Z}'\mathbf{Z})^{-1}\mathbf{Z}' - \mathbf{C}'\mathbf{Z}' - \mathbf{ZC} + \mathbf{C}'\mathbf{Z}'\mathbf{ZC}]\mathbf{y}.$$ separating terms

The first term in this last line does not depend on $\mathbf{C}$, so as our objective is to choose $\mathbf{C}$ to minimise S we concentrate on the second term. Here the matrix expression in square brackets can be factorised:

$$\mathbf{Z}(\mathbf{Z}'\mathbf{Z})^{-1}\mathbf{Z}' - \mathbf{C}'\mathbf{Z}' - \mathbf{ZC} + \mathbf{C}'\mathbf{Z}'\mathbf{ZC} =$$
$$[\mathbf{Z}(\mathbf{Z}'\mathbf{Z})^{-1}\mathbf{Z}' - \mathbf{C}'\mathbf{Z}'][\mathbf{Z}(\mathbf{Z}'\mathbf{Z})^{-1}\mathbf{Z}' - \mathbf{ZC}] = \mathbf{A}'\mathbf{A}, \text{ say.}$$

(In multiplying out to check this, you will find that $\mathbf{Z}'\mathbf{Z}$ matrices cancel out with $(\mathbf{Z}'\mathbf{Z})^{-1}$.) Thus the second term in the expression for S can be written $\mathbf{y}'\mathbf{A}'\mathbf{A}\mathbf{y}$, where $\mathbf{A} = \mathbf{Z}(\mathbf{Z}'\mathbf{Z})^{-1}\mathbf{Z}' - \mathbf{ZC}$ is a $T \times T$

matrix. But $\mathbf{Ay}$ is a T-element column vector, and $\mathbf{y'A'Ay} = (\mathbf{Ay})'(\mathbf{Ay})$ is the sum of squares of the elements of $\mathbf{Ay}$, which has a minimum value of zero – it cannot be negative. This minimum will be achieved when every element of $\mathbf{A}$ is zero, that is, when $\mathbf{Z(Z'Z)^{-1}Z' = ZC}$. So this determines the matrix $\mathbf{C}$ which minimises S, and we have the least squares estimate

$$\mathbf{p} = (\mathbf{Z'Z})^{-1}\mathbf{Z'y}$$

with (minimised) residual sum of squares

$$\Sigma\hat{v}_t^2 = \mathbf{y'}[\mathbf{I}-\mathbf{Z}(\mathbf{Z\,Z})^{-1}\mathbf{Z'}]\mathbf{y} \qquad (2)$$

Had we proceeded by differentiating S with respect to $\mathbf{p}$ and setting the resulting derivatives equal to zero, we would have obtained the normal equations of least squares in the form

$$\mathbf{Z'y} = \mathbf{Z'Zp},$$

generalising those presented on p.70 for the simple regression case, and their solution yields the least squares estimator $\mathbf{p}$ just presented.

The $\mathbf{Z'Z}$ matrix is often referred to as a moment matrix, for when we are working with data in mean deviation form, the elements of $\mathbf{Z'Z}$ are the moments defined on p.71, say $m_{ij} = \Sigma(z_{it}-\bar{z}_i)(z_{jt}-\bar{z}_j)$. The matrix is, of course, symmetric.

The *bias* and *consistency* properties of $\mathbf{p}$ are the same as in the simple case, summarised in tables on pages 73 and 77. As an illustration of the method of proof, we show unbiasedness in the case of exogenous $\mathbf{Z}$.

$$\mathbf{p} = (\mathbf{Z'Z})^{-1}\mathbf{Z'y} = (\mathbf{Z'Z})^{-1}\mathbf{Z'}(\mathbf{Z}\pi+\mathbf{v}) = \pi + (\mathbf{Z'Z})^{-1}\mathbf{Z'v}$$

$$\begin{aligned}
\text{Therefore} \quad E(\mathbf{p}) &= \pi + E(\mathbf{Z'Z})^{-1}\mathbf{Z'v} \\
&= \pi + E(\mathbf{Z'Z})^{-1}\mathbf{Z'}E(\mathbf{v}) && \text{by independence} \\
&= \pi && \text{since } E(\mathbf{v}) = 0.
\end{aligned}$$

An unbiased estimate w^2 of ω^2, the variance of the error term is given by dividing the residual sum of squares by the degrees of freedom remaining after estimation (the sample size, T, minus the number of estimated coefficients K)

$$\text{i.e.} \qquad w^2 = \frac{\Sigma\hat{v}_t^2}{T-K} = \frac{\hat{\mathbf{v}}'\hat{\mathbf{v}}}{T-K}.$$

The *partition* of the original sum of squares goes through as before. From (2) we have

$$\mathbf{y'y} = \mathbf{y'Z}(\mathbf{Z'Z})^{-1}\mathbf{Z'y} + \hat{\mathbf{v}}'\hat{\mathbf{v}}$$

and the first term on the right hand side is the explained sum of squares $\hat{\mathbf{y}}'\hat{\mathbf{y}}$, since $\hat{\mathbf{y}} = \mathbf{Zp}$ and

$$\hat{\mathbf{y}}'\hat{\mathbf{y}} = \mathbf{p'Z'Zp} = \mathbf{y'Z}(\mathbf{Z'Z})^{-1}\mathbf{Z'Z}(\mathbf{Z'Z})^{-1}\mathbf{Z'y} = \mathbf{y'Z}(\mathbf{Z'Z})^{-1}\mathbf{Z'y}.$$

Here it does make a difference whether the data are in original or mean deviation form – if the latter, the above relationship is alright, giving a partition of the original sum of squares around the mean or, if divided through by T, a partition of the original variance. In order to achieve the same interpretation for data not in mean deviation form we have to correct for the mean, and the original sum of squares is $\Sigma(y_t - \bar{y})^2 = \mathbf{y}'\mathbf{y} - T\bar{y}^2$. It is still true that $\bar{y} = \bar{\hat{y}}$, and so the same correction serves for the sum of squares due to regression $\Sigma(\hat{y}_t - \bar{y})^2$ and the equation becomes

$$\mathbf{y}'\mathbf{y} - T\bar{y}^2 = (\hat{\mathbf{y}}'\hat{\mathbf{y}} - T\bar{y}^2) + \hat{\mathbf{v}}'\hat{\mathbf{v}}$$

or

$$\mathbf{y}'\mathbf{y} - \frac{(\Sigma y_t)^2}{T} = [\hat{\mathbf{y}}'\hat{\mathbf{y}} - \frac{(\Sigma y_t)^2}{T}] + \hat{\mathbf{v}}'\hat{\mathbf{v}}.$$

This is important when we come to measure *goodness of fit* by computing R^2, for this is the ratio of explained to original sums of squares around the mean. Perhaps it is simplest to state it once and for all in the following terms:

$$R^2 = \frac{\hat{\mathbf{y}}'\hat{\mathbf{y}} - T\bar{y}^2}{\mathbf{y}'\mathbf{y} - T\bar{y}^2} = \frac{\mathbf{y}'\mathbf{y} - T\bar{y}^2 - \hat{\mathbf{v}}'\hat{\mathbf{v}}}{\mathbf{y}'\mathbf{y} - T\bar{y}^2} = 1 - \frac{\Sigma \hat{v}_t^2}{\Sigma(\hat{y}_t - \bar{y})^2}$$

for if the variables are already in mean deviation form we simply have $\bar{y} = 0$ and the correction drops out.

R^2 provides the basis for assessing the overall performance of the regression equation: it tells us how well the z's explain the dependent variable, and it is possible to contruct an F-ratio test of the null hypothesis that the z's have no effect on y. R^2 has the property that it will almost always increase as extra explanatory variables are added into a regression equation – it will never decrease, and at worst will remain the same if the new variable contributes nothing to the explanatory power of the equation. An alternative measure which does not have this property and which is sometimes found in reported empirical work is $\bar{R}^2$, or R^2 corrected for degrees of freedom. This is obtained by expressing the earlier definition in terms of variance rather than sums of squares, i.e. taking 1 minus the residual variance divided by the original variance, and then using unbiased estimates of these variances, thus

$$\bar{R}^2 = 1 - \frac{\frac{1}{T-K}\Sigma \hat{v}_t^2}{\frac{1}{T-1}\Sigma(y_t - \bar{y})^2}.$$

This is easily expressed in terms of uncorrected R^2, for

$$\bar{R}^2 = 1 - \frac{T-1}{T-K}(1-R^2).$$

$\bar{R}^2$ may decrease as new variables are added in, if they contribute little to the overall explanation of the dependent variable. (Personally I have never been very clear about why one looks at $\bar{R}^2$ when a new variable is added in, rather than carrying out a significance test on the coefficient of the new variable. In any case it is possible to show that $\bar{R}^2$ increases or decreases according as the t-ratio for the coefficient of the new variable is greater than or less than 1, which is a rather low target value.)

Tests of regression coefficients

In the simple regression case we considered a t-test of the regression coefficient. The same type of procedure can be generalised to the multiple regression case, where we are interested in testing single coefficients one at a time. R^2 measures the goodness of fit of the regression as a whole, but it is possible for a well-fitting regression to contain some insignificant coefficients.

The previous notion of the variance of a simple regression coefficient generalises to the *variance–covariance matrix* of the vector **p**, defined as the $K \times K$ matrix $E(\mathbf{p}-\pi)(\mathbf{p}-\pi)'$. This symmetric matrix contains the variances of the p_k on its main diagonal and covariances everywhere else:

$$E(\mathbf{p}-\pi)(\mathbf{p}-\pi)' = \begin{bmatrix} \text{var}\, p_1 & \text{cov}(p_1,p_2) & \ldots & \text{cov}(p_1,p_K) \\ \text{cov}(p_1,p_2) & \text{var}\, p_2 & & \\ \cdot & & & \\ \cdot & & & \\ \cdot & & & \text{var}\, p_K \end{bmatrix}$$

When we come to test coefficients we shall generally be concerned with the elements in the main diagonal but there are situations in which the covariances are of interest too. In the simple regression case we needed to assume serial independence of the error terms for the derivation of the variance of the regression coefficient. This is also required here, and can be conveniently expressed in terms of the variance-covariance matrix of the ν's:

$$E(\mathbf{vv}') = E\begin{bmatrix} \nu_1^2 & \nu_1\nu_2 & \cdot\ \cdot\ \cdot & \nu_1\nu_T \\ \nu_1\nu_2 & \nu_2^2 & & \\ \cdot & & \cdot & \\ \cdot & & \cdot & \\ \cdot & & \cdot & \\ \nu_1\nu_T & & & \nu_T^2 \end{bmatrix}$$

The non-autocorrelation assumption implies that all off-diagonal elements have zero expected value, and the assumption that the variance of ν is constant over time (homoscedasticity) implies that the diagonal elements have expected value ω^2, hence under these conditions

$$E(\mathbf{vv}') = \omega^2 \mathbf{I}$$

where $\mathbf{I}$ is the $T \times T$ unit matrix. Now

$$E(\mathbf{p}-\pi)(\mathbf{p}-\pi)' = E[(\mathbf{Z}'\mathbf{Z})^{-1}\mathbf{Z}'\mathbf{v}]\,[\mathbf{v}'\mathbf{Z}(\mathbf{Z}'\mathbf{Z})^{-1}]$$

(from p.83 above). Taking the z's as a set of fixed numbers or deriving the variance-covariance matrix of $\mathbf{p}$ conditional upon the observed values of the z's, we have

$$\begin{aligned} E(\mathbf{p}-\pi)(\mathbf{p}-\pi)' &= (\mathbf{Z}'\mathbf{Z})^{-1}\mathbf{Z}'.\mathrm{E}(\mathbf{vv}').\mathbf{Z}(\mathbf{Z}'\mathbf{Z})^{-1} \\ &= (\mathbf{Z}'\mathbf{Z})^{-1}\mathbf{Z}'.\omega^2\mathbf{I}.\mathbf{Z}(\mathbf{Z}'\mathbf{Z})^{-1} \quad \text{under the above assumption} \\ &= \omega^2(\mathbf{Z}'\mathbf{Z})^{-1}\mathbf{Z}'\mathbf{Z}(\mathbf{Z}'\mathbf{Z})^{-1} \\ &= \omega^2(\mathbf{Z}'\mathbf{Z})^{-1} \end{aligned}$$

(Note that in the simple regression case, where the matrix $\mathbf{Z}$ has only one column containing the variable z_t, $t=1,\ldots,T$, in mean deviation form, this expression reduces to the scalar quantity $\omega^2/\Sigma(z_t-\bar{z})^2$ derived on p.75.) The variances of the regression coefficients are given by the diagonal elements of this matrix, and under the assumed conditions ($E(\mathbf{v}) = \mathbf{0}$, $E(\mathbf{vv}') = \omega^2\mathbf{I}$, exogenous $\mathbf{Z}$) it is possible to show that these variances are the smallest of any unbiased estimator, and hence that OLS estimates are *best* linear unbiased estimates. The variances are estimated by replacing the unknown ω^2 by the estimate w^2 defined above (p.83), and the *standard error* (estimated standard deviation) of a regression coefficient p_k is given by

$$SE(p_k) = w\sqrt{k\text{th diagonal element of } (\mathbf{Z}'\mathbf{Z})^{-1}}$$

From this formula t-ratios and tests of hypotheses immediately follow as before (p.79). If the null hypothesis of interest is $H_0: \pi_k = 0$ then we compare the ratio $p_k/SE(p_k)$ with the tabulated percentage points of the t distribution with $T-K$ degrees of freedom.

To anticipate the discussion of autocorrelation, let us note its effect on the above derivation of the covariance matrix of $\mathbf{p}$. If the error term is autocorrelated, $E(\mathbf{vv}')$ is no longer diagonal (i.e. $E(v_t v_s) \neq 0$) and we replace the particular matrix $\omega^2\mathbf{I}$ by the general $T \times T$ matrix

$$E(\mathbf{vv}') = \Lambda.$$

The second stage in the derivation of the covariance matrix of $\mathbf{p}$ now becomes

$$E(\mathbf{p}-\pi)(\mathbf{p}-\pi)' = (\mathbf{Z}'\mathbf{Z})^{-1}\mathbf{Z}'\Lambda\mathbf{Z}(\mathbf{Z}'\mathbf{Z})^{-1}$$

which does not simplify any further. These variances are no longer the smallest possible – the OLS estimates are no longer best linear unbiased in the presence of autocorrelated errors. Also calculating standard errors by the previous formula will give biased answers, for they are based on the wrong covariance matrix. We shall return to these points in section 5.4.

The nature of the **Z'Z** *matrix: multicollinearity*

We briefly consider two special cases, and then the problem of multicollinearity. We assume that all variables are given in mean deviation form.

1. If the z variables are mutually uncorrelated, having zero cross-products, then **Z'Z** is simply a diagonal matrix

$$\mathbf{Z'Z} = \begin{bmatrix} \Sigma z_{1t}^2 & \cdot & 0 \\ & \cdot & \\ 0 & \cdot & \Sigma z_{Kt}^2 \end{bmatrix}$$

Its inverse is also diagonal, with elements given by the reciprocals of these diagonal elements. So in calculating regression coefficients $\mathbf{p} = (\mathbf{Z'Z})^{-1}\mathbf{Z'y}$, the only non-zero element in the kth row of $(\mathbf{Z'Z})^{-1}$ is the kth element $1/\Sigma z_{kt}^2$ and this multiplied by the kth element of the vector $\mathbf{Z'y}$ gives

$$p_k = \frac{\Sigma z_{kt} y_t}{\Sigma z_{kt}^2}$$

the simple regression coefficient. Equally, $\text{var}(p_k) = \omega^2/\Sigma z_{kt}^2$ corresponds to the simple regression case. So although in general multiple regression coefficients and simple regression coefficients differ, in the situation where the explanatory variables are uncorrelated, the multiple regression coefficients are precisely the same as the simple regression coefficients – i.e. the coefficients obtained in K simple regressions, taking the explanatory variables one at a time. This situation is somewhat unusual, and the typical situation is one in which the z's are correlated.

2. We first consider the opposite extreme to the preceding case, in which we have perfect correlations or exact linear relationships among the explanatory variables. In this case **Z'Z** is singular, so that $(\mathbf{Z'Z})^{-1}$ does not exist, and it is not possible to calculate K regression coefficients. At best, the number of coefficients which can be calculated is K less the number of linear relations among the variables, and the resulting coefficients are linear functions of the original coefficients. For example, with the equation

$$y_t = \pi_1 z_{1t} + \pi_2 z_{2t} + v_t,$$

suppose that z_1 and z_2 are perfectly correlated, with $z_{1t} = \lambda z_{2t}$, $t = 1,\ldots,T$. Then π_1 and π_2 cannot be separately estimated. On substituting in to obtain

$$y_t = (\pi_1 + \frac{1}{\lambda}\pi_2) z_{1t} + v_t,$$

we see that all we can obtain is an estimate of $(\pi_1 + \frac{1}{\lambda}\pi_2)$. It would be no help to make the other substitution, and estimate $(\lambda\pi_1 + \pi_2)$ in the equation

$$y_t = (\lambda\pi_1 + \pi_2)z_{2t} + v_t,$$

for the estimated coefficient would simply be λ times the coefficient obtained in regressing y on z_1, providing no additional information about the separate values of π_1 and π_2.

3. The problem of multicollinearity arises as we approach this extreme case, so that the z's are highly but not perfectly correlated and the determinant of $\mathbf{Z'Z}$ is small but not zero. OLS estimates can still be calculated, and remain unbiased if the z's are exogenous, but the coefficients are less reliable for their variances and covariances increase. In the case of non-autocorrelated errors the variance-covariance matrix of $\mathbf{p}$ is given by $\omega^2(\mathbf{Z'Z})^{-1}$, and the elements of this matrix will be large if $\mathbf{Z'Z}$ has a determinant close to zero.

Taking the case of two explanatory variables by way of illustration:

$$\begin{bmatrix} p_1 \\ p_2 \end{bmatrix} = \begin{bmatrix} \Sigma z_{1t}^2 & \Sigma z_{1t}z_{2t} \\ \Sigma z_{1t}z_{2t} & \Sigma z_{2t}^2 \end{bmatrix}^{-1} \begin{bmatrix} \Sigma z_{1t}\, y_t \\ \Sigma z_{2t}\, y_t \end{bmatrix},$$

and inverting the $\mathbf{Z'Z}$ matrix to give the covariance matrix of the p's:

$$E(\mathbf{p}-\pi)(\mathbf{p}-\pi)' = \begin{bmatrix} \operatorname{var}(p_1) & \operatorname{cov}(p_1,p_2) \\ \operatorname{cov}(p_1,p_2) & \operatorname{var}(p_2) \end{bmatrix}$$

$$= \frac{\omega^2}{\Sigma z_{1t}^2 \Sigma z_{2t}^2 - (\Sigma z_{1t}z_{2t})^2} \begin{bmatrix} \Sigma z_{2t}^2 & -\Sigma z_{1t}z_{2t} \\ -\Sigma z_{1t}z_{2t} & \Sigma z_{1t}^2 \end{bmatrix}$$

If r_{12} is the coefficient of correlation between z_1 and z_2 then we can write the diagonal elements as follows:

$$\operatorname{var}(p_1) = \frac{\omega^2}{(1-r_{12}^2)\Sigma z_{1t}^2}, \qquad \operatorname{var}(p_2) = \frac{\omega^2}{(1-r_{12}^2)\Sigma z_{2t}^2}.$$

So the variances are larger the closer r_{12} is to 1, and the consequence of a high correlation between explanatory variables is that the coefficients are less precisely determined. Also the covariances increase, and in this case the covariance of the two coefficients is of the opposite sign to the covariance of the two explanatory variables; specifically, the correlation between $(p_1-\pi_1)$ and $(p_2-\pi_2)$ is $-r_{12}$. Thus if z_1 and z_2 are positively correlated, the sampling errors in p_1 and p_2 are negatively correlated. The OLS estimates cannot distinguish too clearly between the effects of z_1 and z_2, which move together, and so to keep the regression passing through the point of sample means, a negative sampling error in p_1 tends to be associated with a positive sampling error in p_2, and vice versa. Notice that, as usual, the variances decrease as the sample size increases, for this increases the number of terms in the sum of squares in the denominator of the above expressions.

For more than two explanatory variables it is not possible to give this kind of intuitive illustration; it remains true, however, that variances and covariances of coefficients increase as the correlation between the z's increases. An illustrative but not uncommon situation, often referred to as a 'problem of multicollinearity', is that in which two explanatory variables are almost perfect substitutes for each other. Enter either of the variables into the regression equation and its coefficient is significant, R^2 being the same whichever variable is used. Put both of them into theequation and one appears highly significant and the other non-significant, their coefficients perhaps changing substantially from the earlier values, but R^2 hardly increasing at all. As we have seen, these phenomena result from high correlations between explanatory variables. In this situation, it is over-optimistic to expect a small sample of data to provide the answer to the question "which variable is the 'right' one?" Since the advice to go and collect more data is usually impractical, all that one can suggest is that more a priori information is needed – a return to economics from statistics. The sample of data on the two correlated variables is not providing enough information, and more must be sought – from economic theory if no other source is available.

5.4 *Autocorrelation*

We now consider the possibility that the errors of a reduced form equation estimated from time series data are autocorrelated. It is no longer true that the covariance matrix of the v's is equal to a scalar product of the unit matrix i.e. $E(\mathbf{vv}') \neq \omega^2 \mathbf{I}$, or equivalently $E(v_t v_s) \neq 0$.

How does autocorrelation arise? We can distinguish two situations. First, recall the conventional rationalisation for including a random error term in an economic model – exact models do not account for the observations, and discrepancies between observations and the predictions of exact theory are accounted for by the error term. This is taken to represent the influence of omitted variables (those that cannot be measured or observed or identified) on the dependent variable. If it is the case that some of these omitted variables behave like observable economic variables than we will expect to find an autocorrelated pattern in them, for most economic time series exhibit autocorrelation. Thus v_t depends on its own past values. In this situation what we usually do is adopt the simplest possible hypothesis to account for serially dependent errors, namely the first order autoregressive scheme:

$$v_t = \rho v_{t-1} + \epsilon_t, \quad -1 < \rho < 1.$$

The ϵ's have zero mean, $E(\epsilon_t) = 0$, (hence so do the ν's) and are independent random variables, $E(\epsilon_t \epsilon_s) = 0$ for $t \neq s$. The covariance matrix of the ν's is then

$$E(\mathbf{vv}') = \Lambda = \omega^2 \begin{bmatrix} 1 & \rho & \rho^2 & \cdots & \rho^{T-1} \\ \rho & 1 & \rho & & \vdots \\ \rho^2 & \rho & 1 & \ddots & \\ \vdots & & \ddots & \ddots & \\ \rho^{T-1} & & & & 1 \end{bmatrix}$$

Secondly, autocorrelated errors may result from transformations of structural equations into their final form prior to estimation. This can be illustrated by reconsidering one of the distributed lag models of section 3.5 in stochastic form. Consider the relationship

$$y_t = \alpha + \beta \hat{x}_{t+1} + u_t$$

(where y_t might be an inventory level and $\hat{x}_{t+1}$ forecast sales in the next period). The adaptive expectations hypothesis

$$\hat{x}_{t+1} = \gamma \hat{x}_t + (1-\gamma) x_t$$

results in the equation (see p.35)

$$y_t = \alpha + \beta (1-\gamma) \sum_{j=0}^{\infty} \gamma^j x_{t-j} + u_t .$$

Then the Koyck transformation eliminates the infinite lag. (Even if we tried to estimate this equation directly we would expect to find multicollinearity among the lagged values of x.) This yields

$$y_t = \alpha(1-\gamma) + \gamma y_{t-1} + \beta(1-\gamma) x_t + (u_t - \gamma u_{t-1}).$$

What is of interest in the present context is the form of the error term $\nu_t = u_t - \gamma u_{t-1}$. Even though we may have started out with non-autocorrelated errors in the first behavioural relationship, it is no longer true here for ν_t is a moving average of the u's. Hence if we look at the first-order autocovariance of the ν's it will not be zero even if $E(u_t u_{t-1}) = 0$. That is,

$$E(\nu_t \nu_{t-1}) = E(u_t - \gamma u_{t-1})(u_{t-1} - \gamma u_{t-2}) = -\gamma \operatorname{var}(u)$$

if u is itself an independent series. And if u is itself autocorrelated, the situation is more complex. (There is a special case where $E(\nu_t \nu_{t-1}) = 0$ – if the original structural disturbance is itself first order autoregressive with the parameter γ (i.e. the expectations parameter): $u_t = \gamma u_{t-1} + \epsilon_t$. This situation seems extremely unlikely to hold.) You might check that if an error term u_t^* is added to the equation for $\hat{x}_{t+1}$ then it also appears in the error term of the final equation, which becomes $u_t - \gamma u_{t-1} + \beta u_t^*$. The general conclusion, that the residuals of this equation can be expected to exhibit autocorrelation, is unchanged. The fact that the serial correlation parameter is also a parameter of the model complicates the estimation problem – we discuss it no further. It simply serves here to indicate that serial correlation of the errors can be introduced in solving dynamic systems.

The partial adjustment model does not have this property of autocorrelated errors induced by a transformation. Though we said (p.37) that the adaptive expectations and partial adjustment models had the same final form, if one had a very fine estimating technique one might be able to distinguish these two hypotheses from each other on the basis of the error term, but if the original structural disturbances were autocorrelated this would be virtually impossible.

Consequences of autocorrelation

What are the consequences for the properties of the estimates if one is using ordinary least squares on a reduced form equation with autocorrelated errors?

The first case to dispose of is that when lagged endogenous variables are present on the right hand side. Least squares estimates are then neither unbiased nor even consistent, as noted earlier and estimation in this case is not easy*.

A slightly easier case to treat is that of exogenous explanatory variables. OLS estimates then remain unbiased in the presence of autocorrelated errors. However, they are no longer the 'best' (minimum variance) estimator. Technically, we say there is a loss of efficiency: there is some other estimator with a smaller sampling variance, to which we shall come below. Further, as indicated above (p.86), the way in which variances and covariances of OLS estimates are calculated assuming serial independence underestimates the true variances if errors are autocorrelated. That is, in the least squares calculations, it is assumed that $E(\mathbf{p}-\pi)(\mathbf{p}-\pi)'=\omega^2(\mathbf{Z}'\mathbf{Z})^{-1}$, whereas the true covariance matrix of OLS estimates now is $(\mathbf{Z}'\mathbf{Z})^{-1}\mathbf{Z}'\Lambda\mathbf{Z}(\mathbf{Z}'\mathbf{Z})^{-1}$, and we will be inclined to be over-optimistic about the significance of coefficients. Finally, applying OLS formulae as if the errors are not autocorrelated leads to an underestimate of the error variance (ω^2) when they are, and so we also get an overoptimistic R^2

Testing for autocorrelation

Given these consequences it is clearly important to test for the presence of autocorrelation in the errors. One difficulty is that the

*For a suggested procedure, see K. F. Wallis, "Lagged Dependent Variables and Serially Correlated Errors", *Review of Economics and Statistics*, November 1967.

assumptions about the form of autocorrelation are stated in relation to the ν's which are unobserved. We therefore have to work with the estimated errors, the regression residuals $\hat{\nu}_t$.

The standard test employs the Durbin-Watson statistic – the ratio of the sum of squares of the first differences of the residuals to their sum of squares:

$$d = \frac{\sum_{t=2}^{T} (\hat{\nu}_t - \hat{\nu}_{t-1})^2}{\sum_{t=1}^{T} \hat{\nu}_t^2}$$

In order to see what is going on when we use this as a test statistic we expand the numerator:

$$d = \frac{\sum_{t=2}^{T} (\hat{\nu}_t^2 + \hat{\nu}_{t-1}^2 - 2\hat{\nu}_t\hat{\nu}_{t-1})}{\sum_{t=1}^{T} \hat{\nu}_t^2}$$

The first two terms in the numerator are almost the same as the denominator, the only difference is that the terms in the numerator contain $T-1$ squared residuals, whereas the denominator is the sum of squares of all T residuals. Neglecting this difference, we have

$$d \cong 2(1 - \frac{\Sigma\hat{\nu}_t\hat{\nu}_{t-1}}{\Sigma\hat{\nu}_t^2}).$$

Here the second term is close to what we take as our least squares estimator of ρ if we have the first order autoregressive process in the errors $\nu_t = \rho\nu_{t-1} + \epsilon_t$, and use the residuals $\hat{\nu}_t$ in place of the unobserved errors. So

$$d \cong 2(1 - \hat{\rho})$$

where $\hat{\rho}$ is the first order autocorrelation coefficient of the residuals. Therefore if we have zero autocorrelation, $\rho = 0$ and we expect $d = 2$. If the autocorrelation is positive, $0 < \rho < 1$, then $0 < d < 2$, and for negative autocorrelation, $-1 < \rho < 0$ we expect $2 < d < 4$.

Once we have calculated a value of d we want to decide whether this value is sufficiently far away from 2 to force us to reject the hypothesis of independence. So we test the null hypothesis that the errors are independent by comparing the calculated d with tabulated significance points.

There are two points to be made about the Durbin-Watson tables. First, they assume that we are interested in testing against an alternative of positive autocorrelation and so we are expecting (if anything) that the calculated value will be below 2—that is, the test is one-sided. Secondly, the distribution of d depends on the particular regression (explanatory) variables in the estimated equation. And of course when the statistic is tabulated it is not known what variables a researcher will be working with. What Durbin and Watson were able to do was to calculate upper and lower bounds (d_U and d_L) to the distribution's significance points so that, no matter what the nature of the exogenous variables, the true significance point of d lies between d_L and d_U. Therefore if one's calculated d is less than d_L it is probably too low to be explained by sampling variation alone and the null hypothesis of independence is rejected. Equally if the value is between d_U and 2 then the null hypothesis is accepted—such a small departure from 2 can be accounted for by sampling error in a situation of no autocorrelation. If the computed d lies between d_L and d_U the test is unfortunately inconclusive. Most regression variables in economics are such that the actual distribution will be closer to the upper than the lower bound, so that when d falls in the inconclusive region one should nevertheless proceed with caution. If one is interested in the possibility of negative autocorrelation the tabulated significance points must be subtracted from 4, as d now varies between 2 and 4. Then, if the calculated d lies between 2 and $4-d_U$ the null hypothesis is accepted. If d lies between $4-d_L$ and 4 there is evidence of significant negative autocorrelation. Finally, if the calculated d falls between $4-d_U$ and $4-d_L$ the test is again inconclusive.

The Durbin-Watson statistic only tests for first order autocorrelation, the assumption being that, even if one had some higher order autoregressive scheme, the first order autocorrelation coefficient would show up significant. Although this need not necessarily be the case, the assumption does seem quite reasonable when annual data are being employed. (The Durbin-Watson work was done at Cambridge at the time that Stone was estimating demand equations from annual data.) With quarterly data one might wish to consider the possibility that $v_t = \rho v_{t-4} + \epsilon_t$, i.e. that the current regression residual is correlated with that of the same quarter last year rather than that of the previous quarter. It turns out that it is not too difficult to generalise the whole procedure.

Finally, it should be noted that the test is designed for use in regression equations with exogenous explanatory variables. In the presence of the lagged dependent variable, the statistic is biased towards 2, and hence gives overoptimistic answers.

Procedures for dealing with autocorrelation

The question now arises of what to do if we find that the Durbin-Watson test suggests that the errors are autocorrelated. Consider the simple regression equation

$$y_t = \alpha + \pi z_t + v_t$$

where v_t follows the first order autoregressive scheme,

$$v_t = \rho v_{t-1} + \epsilon_t.$$

Lagging the equation and multiplying through by ρ we obtain

$$\rho y_{t-1} = \rho\alpha + \rho\pi z_{t-1} + \rho v_{t-1}$$

and on subtraction we have

$$\begin{aligned} y_t - \rho y_{t-1} &= \alpha(1-\rho) + \pi(z_t - \rho z_{t-1}) + v_t - \rho v_{t-1} \\ &= \alpha(1-\rho) + \pi(z_t - \rho z_{t-1}) + \epsilon_t. \end{aligned}$$

The error term in this equation, ϵ_t, is non-autocorrelated, indeed the equation satisfies the standard least squares assumptions. So if we regress the new dependent variable $(y_t - \rho y_{t-1})$ on the new independent variable $(z_t - \rho z_{t-1})$ using ordinary least squares the resulting estimates are best (minimum variance) linear unbiased once again. (These estimates are very close to those obtained by (Aitken's) generalised least squares, which provides best linear unbiased estimates for the case of $E(\mathbf{vv}') \neq \omega^2\,\mathbf{I}$).

The difficulty with this programme of action is that typically ρ is unknown. An estimate $\hat{\rho}$ must be obtained, and one possibility is to derive this from the Durbin-Watson statistic, because $d \cong 2\,(1-\hat{\rho})$. We then regress the transformed variable $y_t - \hat{\rho} y_{t-1}$ on $z_t - \hat{\rho} z_{t-1}$. This procedure is then successful in that it provides consistent and (asymptotically) efficient estimators provided that z_t is exogenous. If z_t is lagged endogenous then $\hat{\rho}$ will be biased and inconsistent as noted above since it is calculated from ordinary least squares residuals and OLS estimates are themselves biased and inconsistent in this case.

Notice that direct estimation of the transformed equation is not helpful. Collecting all terms except y_t on the right hand side gives

$$y_t = \alpha(1-\rho) + \rho y_{t-1} + \pi z_t - \pi\rho z_{t-1} + \epsilon_t,$$

and one might proceed to a regression of y_t on y_{t-1}, z_t and z_{t-1} (the error term is non-autocorrelated). However, an identification problem arises because the four coefficients are functions of only three parameters, and unique estimates of α, π and ρ cannot be deduced. For example, there is no guarantee that the product of the coefficient of y_{t-1} and the coefficient of z_t will be equal to the negative of the coefficient of z_{t-1} in practice.

The fact that regression using 'quasi-differenced' variables $y_t - \rho y_{t-1}$, etc., has good properties, and the suspicion that with annual data ρ may be close to 1 led to the use of first differences by Stone and others. That is,

$$
\begin{aligned}
& y_t = \alpha + \pi z_t \quad + v_t \\
& y_{t-1} = \alpha + \pi z_{t-1} + v_{t-1} \\
\text{therefore} \quad & \Delta y_t = \quad \pi \Delta z_t + \Delta v_t
\end{aligned}
$$

and Δv_t will be close to ϵ_t if ρ is close to 1. Note that the constant term drops out and the equation should be estimated with a zero intercept. If a constant term is estimated it is equivalent to adding a linear time trend to the original equation. We can show this as follows. If the original equation is $y_t = \alpha_1 + \alpha_2 t + \pi z_t + v_t$, then $y_{t-1} = \alpha_1 + \alpha_2 (t-1) + \pi z_{t-1} + v_{t-1}$, and subtracting gives $\Delta y_t = \alpha_2 + \pi \Delta z_t + \Delta v_t$. The original constant term α_1, disappears, and the intercept term in the first difference equation is the trend coefficient α_2 in the original equation.

Note that we can test whether the first difference procedure is working by again using the Durbin-Watson test in the usual way. If ρ is positive but not equal to 1, then Δv_t will have negative autocorrelation, for which we can test – the smaller ρ the stronger the negative autocorrelation in Δv_t (cf. Exercise 5.6).

5.5 *Least squares and structural equations*

So far we have confined the discussion to estimation of reduced form equations. Next we examine the consequences of applying ordinary least squares to structural equations. It turns out that in general one no longer gets unbiased or consistent estimates, and this problem is known as least squares bias or simultaneous equation bias. Having discussed the problem we shall present alternative methods of estimation which get around it.

Let us take the case of a simple structural equation

$$y_{1t} = \alpha + \beta y_{2t} + u_t$$

–now the equation contains more than one endogenous variable. Let us look at the OLS estimate of β:

$$b = \frac{\Sigma(y_{1t} - \bar{y}_1)(y_{2t} - \bar{y}_2)}{\Sigma(y_{2t} - \bar{y}_2)^2} = \frac{m_{y_1, y_2}}{m_{y_2, y_2}}$$

Expressing the original equation in mean deviation form we have

$$y_{1t} - \bar{y}_1 = \beta(y_{2t} - \bar{y}_2) + (u_t - \bar{u})$$

$$\text{and so } b = \frac{\Sigma[\beta(y_{2t} - \bar{y}_2) + (u_t - \bar{u})](y_{2t} - \bar{y}_2)}{\Sigma(y_{2t} - \bar{y}_2)^2}$$

$$= \beta + \frac{\Sigma(y_{2t} - \bar{y}_2)(u_t - \bar{u})}{\Sigma(y_{2t} - \bar{y}_2)^2} = \beta + \frac{m_{y_2 u}}{m_{y_2 y_2}}$$

This is an exact result, and the sampling error $b-\beta$ could be calculated if the u's were observable. Since y_2 is not a predetermined variable (independent of u) the second term does not have an expected value of zero hence $E(b) \neq \beta$, and b is a biased estimate.

But can anything be discovered about m_{uy_2}? Can we work out the likely size or sign of the discrepancy between b and β?

1. Let us first try without specifying a complete model. Let $y_1 = \log q$ and $y_2 = \log p$ then $\log q = \alpha + \beta \log p + u$ is a supply curve with constant elasticity β. This is illustrated in the diagram for values of β less than, equal to, or greater than one. Remember that, thanks to Marshall, the axes are reversed and the dependent variable is measured on the horizontal axis. Similarly, the error term is a horizontal displacement, and a positive value u_t has the effect of swinging the curve to the right, as illustrated.

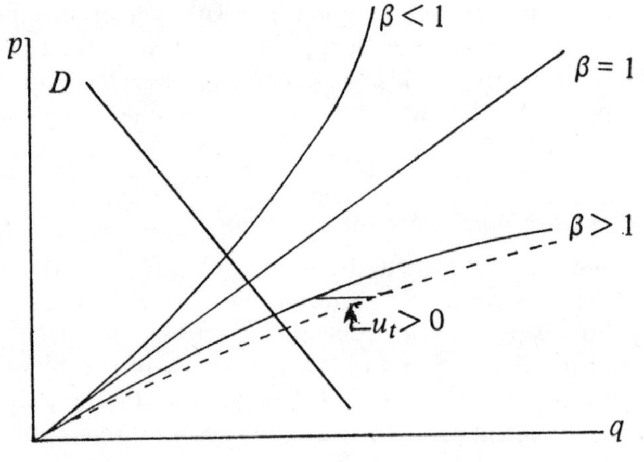

How does this affect our observations? Suppose we superimpose a demand function. Clearly the intersection of D and S shifts so that a positive value of u_t causes the observed price to fall below what it would otherwise be, likewise observed quantity increases. The same result holds irrespective of $\beta \gtrless 1$. Similarly a negative value of the error term in the supply equation causes a higher price and smaller quantity than otherwise to be observed. Hence we find that m_{uy_2} is negative because positive errors are associated with downward shifts in price and vice versa. The denominator of $m_{y_2u}/m_{y_2y_2}$ is positive because it is a sum of squares and the numerator is negative so the OLS estimate of the elasticity β will tend to be too low—the actual sampling error is likely to be negative. To get much further than this we would have to evaluate the actual bias, involving the behaviour of the price series and the actual size rather than just the sign of the correlation with u. But we have got somewhere if we are interested simply in whether supply is elastic or inelastic (i.e. $\beta \gtrless 1$), for if we obtain a value $b > 1$ then it is quite likely that $\beta > 1$ and supply is elastic. However, if the estimate of b turned out to be less than 1 we would be uncertain as to whether β was greater than 1 and the estimate b was a substantial underestimate, or whether b was only a moderate underestimate of a true parameter value which was still less than 1.

2. A second approach is to specify a complete model, and note the interactions implied by the other equations. In our example we obtain an exact expression for the asymptotic bias in the least squares estimate of the m.p.c. The consumption function is

$$c_t = \alpha + \beta y_t + u_t \qquad t = 1,\ldots,T$$

and the OLS estimate b of β can be written

$$b = \beta + \frac{m_{uy}}{m_{yy}}.$$

Suppose the model is completed by the income identity

$$y_t = c_t + i_t$$

and the specification that i_t is exogenous. The fact that b is biased, i.e. that m_{yu}/m_{yy} has a non-zero expected value, results from the endogeneity of y. The way in which y depends on u is made quite explicit by the reduced form:

$$c_t = \frac{1}{1-\beta}(\alpha + \beta i_t + u_t)$$

$$y_t = \frac{1}{1-\beta}(\alpha + i_t + u_t).$$

Thus y and u have a non-zero covariance. Converting the second reduced form equation into mean deviation form gives

$$y_t - \bar{y} = \frac{1}{1-\beta}(i_t - \bar{i} + u_t - \bar{u})$$

and we can now express the sample moments m_{uy} and m_{yy} in terms of the exogenous variable and the random error term.

$$m_{yu} = \Sigma(y_t - \bar{y})(u_t - \bar{u})$$

$$= \frac{1}{1-\beta}\Sigma(i_t - \bar{i} + u_t - \bar{u})(u_t - \bar{u}) = \frac{1}{1-\beta}(m_{iu} + m_{uu})$$

$$m_{yy} = \Sigma(y_t - \bar{y})^2 = \left(\frac{1}{1-\beta}\right)^2 \Sigma(i_t - \bar{i} + u_t - \bar{u})^2$$

$$= \left(\frac{1}{1-\beta}\right)^2 (m_{ii} + m_{uu} + 2m_{iu})$$

Therefore $\qquad b-\beta = \dfrac{m_{yu}}{m_{yy}} = \dfrac{(1-\beta)(m_{iu}+m_{uu})}{m_{ii}+m_{uu}+2m_{iu}}.$

Again this is an exact result in terms of sample moments, although u is unobservable. We have difficulty in taking the expected value of this ratio in order to evaluate the bias, but as discussed earlier (p.76) we can consider the situation as $T \rightarrow \infty$ and show that b is an inconsistent estimate. We divide top and bottom by T, and consider them separately. m_{iu}/T is the estimated covariance of i and u, which has expected value of zero as i is exogenous, and m_{uu}/T has expected value equal to the variance of u as T increases. In the denominator m_{ii}/T converges in probability to var(i) and so we have

$$\lim_{T\to\infty} E(b-\beta) = \frac{(1-\beta)\,\mathrm{var}(u)}{\mathrm{var}(i)+\mathrm{var}(u)} = \frac{(1-\beta)\sigma_u^2}{\sigma_i^2+\sigma_u^2}$$

Under the conventional assumption that the marginal propensity to consume is less than one it is clear that the asymptotic bias given by this expression is positive.

Hence we know that the direct least squares estimate of β is biased and inconsistent, and b is (asymptotically) biased upwards. This large sample bias can be used as an approximation to the bias in small samples. But the next question is what can we do to avoid this situation.

5.6 *Consistent estimation of a structural equation: indirect least squares*

How can we get a consistent estimate of the marginal propensity to consume? The difficulty arose because the explanatory variable in the consumption function (y_t) was related to the error term. But this is not a feature of reduced form equations. The possibility that emerges is to estimate the reduced form and then from this attempt to deduce an estimate of the structural parameter.

The reduced form can be written

$$c_t-\bar{c} = \frac{\beta}{1-\beta}(i_t-\bar{i}) + \frac{1}{1-\beta}(u_t-\bar{u})$$

$$y_t-\bar{y} = \frac{1}{1-\beta}(i_t-\bar{i}) + \frac{1}{1-\beta}(u_t-\bar{u})$$

Thus the least squares estimate of the coefficient in the first reduced form equation is given by

$$\left(\frac{\widehat{\beta}}{1-\beta}\right) = \frac{m_{ci}}{m_{ii}}$$

The estimate of the coefficient in the reduced form equation for income is given by

$$\widehat{\left(\frac{1}{1-\beta}\right)} = \frac{m_{yi}}{m_{ii}}$$

Note that although we have estimates of different functions of β, we can check that the two estimates are consistent with each other. This occurs if

$$\widehat{\left(\frac{1}{1-\beta}\right)} - \widehat{\left(\frac{\beta}{1-\beta}\right)} = 1$$

which requires that $m_{yi} - m_{ci} = m_{ii}$. But this is always true, for the identity $y_t = c_t + i_t$ in mean deviation form

$$y_t - \overline{y} = c_t - \overline{c} + i_t - \overline{i}$$

implies that $\Sigma(y_t - \overline{y})(i_t - \overline{i}) = \Sigma(c_t - \overline{c})(i_t - \overline{i}) + \Sigma(i_t - \overline{i})^2$ (multiplying the equation through by $i_t - \overline{i}$ and summing). That is, $m_{yi} = m_{ci} + m_{ii}$ as required. So it makes no difference which reduced form coefficient we attempt to solve to obtain an estimate of β – the same estimate will result in either case. This is precisely what we would expect from the fact that the consumption function is just-identified, hence the structural parameter values can be deduced uniquely from reduced form coefficient values. So the *indirect least squares* method for a just-identified structural equation is to deduce estimates of its parameters from the estimated reduced form.

In this case we can write the resulting estimate in a slightly simpler form. Taking the first reduced form coefficient, $p_1 = \frac{m_{ci}}{m_{ii}}$, we solve the equation

$$\frac{b}{1-b} = p_1$$

and obtain

$$b = \frac{p_1}{1+p_1}$$

As a consequence of this calculation we have

$$b = \frac{m_{ci}}{m_{ci}+m_{ii}} = \frac{m_{ci}}{m_{yi}}$$

and so the indirect least squares estimate could be calculated straightaway as this ratio of sample moments. This is a simpler form to work with in the next step.

Consistency

Does the indirect least squares estimate have the property of consistency that the direct least squares estimate lacked? To answer the question we again express the elements in the statistic we compute in terms of error terms and exogenous variables, and then use our assumptions about these variables. Multiplying through the reduced form equations at time t by $(i_t - \bar{i})$ and then summing over all T observations gives

$$m_{ci} = \frac{\beta}{1-\beta} m_{ii} + \frac{1}{1-\beta} m_{ui}$$

$$m_{yi} = \frac{1}{1-\beta} m_{ii} + \frac{1}{1-\beta} m_{ui}.$$

Substituting in the expression for b then gives

$$b = \frac{\beta m_{ii} + m_{ui}}{m_{ii} + m_{ui}}$$

Once again we cannot evaluate $E(b)$ in a finite sample case, for a random variable appears in both numerator and denominator. So we may expect that b is generally biased. Does this unknown bias vanish to zero as we increase the sample size? It turns out that it does. In the limit as T becomes large, we can evaluate the top and bottom of the ratio separately. Dividing top and bottom by T the term m_{ui}/T is the sample covariance of u and i, which has zero expected value as i is assumed exogenous. The term m_{ii}/T then cancels out, and the result is that b is an asymptotically unbiased (and consistent) estimate of β.

So we can conclude that the indirect least squares (ILS) technique provides consistent estimates of the parameters of a just-identified structural equation. For the general case let us take the first equation of the model to be the equation of interest (without loss of generality) and, for convenience, drop the first subscript 1 from the coefficients. So the equation to be estimated is

$$y_{1t} + \beta_2 y_{2t} + \ldots + \beta_H y_{Ht} + \gamma_1 z_{1t} + \ldots + \gamma_J z_{Jt} = u_{1t} \qquad t = 1,\ldots,T.$$

We first estimate the reduced form equations for the included endogenous variables. We do this by regressing $y_1, y_2, \ldots, y_H$ in turn on all the exogenous variables $z_1, \ldots, z_K$ obtaining estimated reduced form coefficients p_{ik}, $i=1,\ldots,H$, $k=1,\ldots,K$. From these estimates we deduce estimates of $\beta_2, \ldots, \beta_H$ and $\gamma_1, \ldots, \gamma_J$ by solving equations analogous to those presented on p.62 when we were considering identification. That is, we obtain $\hat{\beta}$'s and $\hat{\gamma}$'s from the equations:

$$
\begin{aligned}
-\hat{\gamma}_1 &= p_{11} &+ \sum_{i=2}^{H} \hat{\beta}_i \, p_{i1} \\
&\;\;\vdots \\
-\hat{\gamma}_J &= p_{1J} &+ \sum_{i=2}^{H} \hat{\beta}_i \, p_{1J} \\
0 &= p_{1,J+1} &+ \sum_{i=2}^{H} \hat{\beta}_i \, p_{i,J+1} \\
&\;\;\vdots \\
0 &= p_{1K} &+ \sum_{i=2}^{H} \hat{\beta}_i \, p_{iK}
\end{aligned}
$$

If the equation is just-identified (K–J = H–1), the second block of K–J equations can be solved for the H–1 parameter estimates $\hat{\beta}_2, \ldots, \hat{\beta}_H$, and the estimates $\hat{\gamma}_1, \ldots, \hat{\gamma}_J$ then follow from the first block of J equations.

If the structural equation is overidentified (K–J > H–1) we have too many equations in the second block, and so we cannot find H–1 $\hat{\beta}$'s which will satisfy all K–J equations. Any H–1 of the K–J equations will yield a solution, but there is more than one way of choosing the H–1 equations to use, and the indirect least squares estimate is not defined for this case. We shall shortly consider estimation of an overidentified equation, but before that we take another look at the just-identified case.

5.7 *The method of instrumental variables*

Return to our just-identified structural equation in mean deviation form:

$$c_t - \bar{c} = \beta(y_t - \bar{y}) + (u_t - \bar{u}).$$

We have shown that the OLS estimate of β is biased and inconsistent. This would be obtained by forming moments with the explanatory variable, giving

$$m_{cy} = \beta m_{yy} + m_{uy} \, ,$$

and then setting $m_{uy} = 0$ to give the least squares normal equation $m_{cy} = b m_{yy}$ yielding an estimate b of β. The method fails because m_{uy} has a non-zero expected value; in the standard least squares situation with exogenous regressors, the normal equations are obtained by setting the moment between the error term and each explanatory variable equal to its expected value of zero.

But what if we form moments with a variable which *is* independent of the error term, i.e. a predetermined variable. The only one in our present model is i_t, and so we have

$$\Sigma(c_t-\bar{c})(i_t-\bar{i}) = \beta\Sigma(y_t-\bar{y})(i_t-\bar{i}) + \Sigma(u_t-\bar{u})(i_t-\bar{i})$$

or $$m_{ci} = \beta m_{yi} + m_{ui}$$

Now u_t and i_t are independent, so $E(m_{ui}) = 0$, and setting m_{ui} equal to its expected value of zero gives the quasi-normal equation

$$m_{ci} = \hat{\beta} m_{yi}.$$

We call i_t an instrumental variable, and the resulting estimate

$$\hat{\beta} = \frac{m_{ci}}{m_{yi}}$$

is the *instrumental variable* (IV) estimate.

We notice immediately that the IV estimate is identical with the ILS estimate (b) derived above (p. 99), and so we expect this estimate to have the same properties. That is, the IV estimate is consistent but not necessarily unbiased.

The general procedure for obtaining IV estimates which we have followed is to form moments with the instrumental (predetermined) variables and derive estimating equations for the coefficients ('quasi-normal' equations) by setting the moments between the instrumental variables and the equation's random error term equal to their expected values of zero. In our example i_t was the instrumental variable: it is a variable of the model and so correlated with all the other variables (in particular $m_{yi} \neq 0$) but it is independent of the error term ($m_{ui} = 0$). There was no problem of choosing an appropriate instrumental variable – we required one such variable in order to form one quasi-normal equation which would give an estimate of the single parameter β, and there was just one predetermined variable available. This is a consequence of the just-identified nature of the equation and in more general situations unique IV estimates can only be obtained for just-identified equations. The order condition for just-identifiability guarantees that there will be the right number of instrumental variables available.

To see this, consider the structural equation

$$y_{1t} + \beta_2 y_{2t} + \dots + \beta_H y_{Ht} + \gamma_1 z_{1t} + \dots + \gamma_J z_{Jt} = u_{1t},$$

which excludes G–H endogenous and K–J predetermined variables. In order to estimate the $H-1$ β's and J γ's we need $H-1+J$ quasi-normal equations. Clearly, it is alright to construct such equations by forming moments with $z_1,\dots,z_J$ in turn, for these are predetermined and independent of u (contemporaneously, at any rate), so these variables can be their own instruments. Endogenous variables cannot be used, however, so we need some other variables to construct cross-products with in place of $y_2,...,y_H$. The remaining candidate variables in the model are $z_{J+1},...,z_K$, which meet the requirements. So we shall be able to form the $H-1+J$ quasi-normal equations if there are just enough excluded predetermined variables available as instruments for the explanatory endogenous variables, i.e. if $K-J = H-1$, or the equation is just-identified. Solution of these equations will yield the IV estimates and, as in the simple example above, these are identical with ILS estimates.

If the equation is over-identified, then $K-J > H-1$, and there are more instrumental variables available than are required, and the problem is how to choose the $H-1$ instrumental variables to use. Equivalently, if we write the condition $K>H-1+J$, then we have more quasi-normal equations than coefficients, and there is not a unique solution for the $\hat{\beta}$'s and $\hat{\gamma}$'s. One might say that the extra equations should be thrown away, and only $H-1+J$ of them used to derive the estimates, but for every way of choosing $H-1+J$ from K there is a different set of IV estimates, and how is one to choose among them? The two stage least squares method overcomes this difficulty by constructing the optimal set of instrumental variables, and this will be our next (and final) estimation method. Before considering this, however, we look at a special case in which OLS estimation of a structural equation can be justified.

5.8 *Recursive systems*

In our discussion of segmentable systems in section 2.5 we described one of the basic requirements for a recursive system, namely that the **B** matrix be triangular. Of course we were then talking about exact systems, and certain definitions (of pre-determined variables, for example) required modification once random error terms were added. The same is true here, and a further requirement is that the errors in the different equations are independent. In general such an assumption has not been made, for the error terms represent the influence of omitted variables, some of which may be common to a number of equations, but now it is necessary. So a *recursive* system is one satisfying two conditions: (i) the matrix of coefficients of the endogenous variables is triangular (possibly after the equations have been re-ordered), and (ii) the errors u_g and u_h, say, are independent in all time periods. The structural equations then form a causal chain, and there are no contemporaneous feedbacks between endogenous variables. The system can be set out as follows, with $E(u_{gt}u_{hs})=0$, $g,h=1,...,G$, $t,s=1,...,T$, (we are taking the most general case in which the z's may be lagged endogenous or purely exogenous variables).

$$
\begin{array}{lr}
y_{1t} & + \sum_{k=1}^{K} \gamma_{1k} z_{kt} = u_{1t} \\
\beta_{21} y_{1t} + \quad y_{2t} & + \sum \gamma_{2k} z_{kt} = u_{2t} \\
\beta_{31} y_{1t} + \beta_{32} y_{2t} + \quad y_{3t} & + \sum \gamma_{3k} z_{kt} = u_{3t} \\
\vdots & \vdots \\
\beta_{G1} y_{1t} + \beta_{G2} y_{2t} + \beta_{G3} y_{3t} + \ldots + y_{Gt} & + \sum \gamma_{Gk} z_{kt} = u_{Gt}
\end{array}
$$

On the face of it, no equation other than the first is identified, the order condition not being met. However it turns out that the restriction of independent errors, of a kind we have not previously considered, will identify the system. Consider the first two equations. The first is identified, excluding $G-1$ variables. The second appears to be unidentified, for adding any multiple of the first to the second produces a new equation containing exactly the same variables. However, the requirement that the first and second structural equations have independent errors is now crucial, for no linear combination of the first and second equations will have an error term independent of u_1, (the linear combination will itself contain u_1). So such a linear combination would not pass as the second equation, which is thereby identified. And so on.

When we come to estimate a particular equation, say the gth, the independent error assumption allows us to regard the endogenous variables $y_1,\ldots,y_{g-1}$ determined in the preceding equations as predetermined with respect to that equation–they are independent of the error term in that equation. Thus the second equation contains only one variable correlated with u_2, namely y_2; the variable y_1 depends on u_1, but u_1 and hence y_1 is independent of u_2. Thus an OLS regression of y_2 on y_1 and the z's will provide consistent estimates of β_{21} and the γ_{2k}'s. Likewise, in the third equation y_1 and y_2 are independent of u_3, and so can be treated as predetermined, the equation being estimated by OLS. These two special requirements, then, of no feedback from higher-numbered to lower-numbered endogenous variables, and of independent errors, eliminate the difficulty found in section 5.5 and allow consistent estimation of structural equations by ordinary least squares.

A simple example is provided by the cobweb model, previously used as an example of a dynamic model. The quantity supplied of a commodity produced in an annual crop depends on the previous year's price; the current price is determined by the demand equation. We write this in triangular form as follows:

$$
\begin{array}{ll}
q_t + & + \gamma p_{t-1} = u_{1t} \\
\beta q_t + p_t & = u_{2t}
\end{array}
$$

The first equation, already being in its reduced form, can be consistently estimated by OLS (we assume the errors to be non-autocorrelated). However, this is only true for the second equation if u_1 and u_2 are independent, whereupon the model becomes recursive. Then q is independent of u_2, and a simple regression of p on q consistently estimates β. If u_1 and u_2 are correlated, we no longer have a recursive system, and OLS is inapplicable. (Since the second equation, excluding p_{t-1}, is just-identified, it might then be appropriately estimated by IV, using p_{t-1} as an instrumental variable for q_t, so that

$$\hat{\beta} = -\frac{\Sigma p_t p_{t-1}}{\Sigma q_t p_{t-1}}.)$$

The recursive assumption might be reasonable here, however, for it could well be the case that none of the variables omitted from the supply equation and appearing in u_1 are also to be found in u_2.

5.9 *Estimation of an overidentified structural equation*

We now leave the special case of the previous section and consider how to estimate a structural equation when it is overidentified. First, however, we introduce some new matrix notation and use it to repeat the preceding discussion of IV estimation.

We adopt the convention used in regression analysis of writing all the explanatory variables on the right hand side. Again, for simplicity but with no loss of generality we assume that we want to estimate the first structural equation in a model. Hence the included endogenous variables are $y_1,...,y_H$ and, normalising on y_1, we write that variable on the left hand side. The endogenous variables $y_{H+1},...,y_G$ and predetermined variables $z_{J+1},...,z_K$ are excluded from the equation, which we write

$$y_{1t} = -(\beta_2 y_{2t} + ... + \beta_H y_{Ht} + \gamma_1 z_{1t} \qquad + \gamma_J z_{Jt}) + u_{1t}, \quad t = 1,...,T.$$

The column vector of observations on the 'dependent' endogenous variable is

$$\mathbf{y} = (y_{11},...,y_{1t})', \qquad \text{and } \mathbf{u} = (u_{11},...,u_{1T})',$$

and the $T \times (H-1)$ matrix of observations on the 'explanatory' endogenous variables is

$$\mathbf{Y} = \begin{bmatrix} y_{21} & y_{31} & \cdots & y_{H1} \\ \cdot & \cdot & & \cdot \\ \cdot & \cdot & & \cdot \\ \cdot & \cdot & & \cdot \\ y_{2T} & y_{3T} & \cdots & y_{HT} \end{bmatrix}$$

In the $T \times K$ matrix $\mathbf{Z}$ of associated observations on the predetermined variables it is important to distinguish the J variables which are included and the $K-J$ which are excluded. Hence we partition the $\mathbf{Z}$ matrix as follows:

$$\mathbf{Z} = \left[\begin{array}{ccc|ccc} z_{11} & \cdots & z_{J1} & z_{J+1,1} & \cdots & z_{K1} \\ \cdot & & \cdot & \cdot & & \cdot \\ \cdot & & \cdot & \cdot & & \cdot \\ \cdot & & \cdot & \cdot & & \cdot \\ z_{1T} & \cdots & z_{JT} & z_{J+1,T} & \cdots & z_{KT} \end{array}\right] = (\mathbf{Z}^* \; \mathbf{Z}\dagger)$$

The vectors of coefficients we wish to estimate are given by

$$\beta = (\beta_2, \ldots, \beta_H)' \qquad \gamma = (\gamma_1, \ldots, \gamma_J)'$$

Note that the β -vector has the first element missing. In this new notation the equation we wish to estimate now appears as follows:

$$\mathbf{y} = -\mathbf{Y}\beta - \mathbf{Z}^*\gamma + \mathbf{u}.$$

We can also set out the IV estimates of a just identified equation, i.e. assuming that the number of excluded predetermined variables is equal to the number of right hand side endogenous variables ($K-J = H-1$). The IV method is precisely equivalent to ordinary least squares except that excluded predetermined variables $\mathbf{Z}\dagger$ are used to form normal equations in place of (that is, as instrumental variables for) the right hand side endogenous variables $\mathbf{Y}$. (If some of the z's are lagged endogenous, we need to assume that u is non-autocorrelated for consistency to hold.) The OLS normal equations, providing estimates shown to be inconsistent in section 5.5, would be (cf. p.83)

$$(\mathbf{Y}\;\mathbf{Z}^*)'\,\mathbf{y} = (\mathbf{Y}\;\mathbf{Z}^*)'\,(\mathbf{Y}\;\mathbf{Z}^*)\begin{bmatrix} -\hat{\beta} \\ -\hat{\gamma} \end{bmatrix}$$

and the instrumental variable normal equations are

$$(\mathbf{Z}\dagger\;\mathbf{Z}^*)'\,\mathbf{y} = (\mathbf{Z}\dagger\;\mathbf{Z}^*)'\,(\mathbf{Y}\;\mathbf{Z}^*)\begin{bmatrix} -\hat{\beta} \\ -\hat{\gamma} \end{bmatrix}$$

So the IV estimates are given by

$$\begin{bmatrix} \hat{\beta} \\ \hat{\gamma} \end{bmatrix} = -\begin{bmatrix} \mathbf{Z}\dagger'\mathbf{Y} & \mathbf{Z}\dagger'\mathbf{Z}^* \\ \mathbf{Z}^{*\prime}\mathbf{Y} & \mathbf{Z}^{*\prime}\mathbf{Z}^* \end{bmatrix}^{-1} \begin{bmatrix} \mathbf{Z}\dagger'\mathbf{y} \\ \mathbf{Z}^{*\prime}\mathbf{y} \end{bmatrix}.$$

The assumption that the equation is just identified by the order condition implies $\mathbf{Z}\dagger$ has $H-1$ columns and hence that all these matrices conform. As mentioned previously, if $K-J > H-1$ and the equation is overidentified, we have too many instrumental variables. Notice that economic theory is no guide to selection in this situation, for the candidate variables $z_{J+1}, \ldots, z_K$ are all predetermined variables of equal standing in our model. The problem of selecting $H-1$ appropriate instruments is resolved by our next estimation method.

Two stage least squares (2SLS)

We assume $K-J > H-1$, and describe the 2SLS method according to Theil's presentation, returning at the end to interpret the method in the instrumental variable framework. Recall that the problem with direct OLS estimation of

$$y_{1t} = -(\beta_2 y_{2t} + \ldots + \beta_H y_{Ht} + \gamma_1 z_{1t} + \ldots + \gamma_J z_{Jt}) + u_{1t}$$

arises from the fact that the right hand side endogenous variables are correlated with the error term. We may ask whether there are any variables that behave like these endogenous variables but do not have this property, i.e. are independent of u. An obvious clue is that the reduced form predictions are uncorrelated with u. If we knew the reduced form values for the right hand side endogenous variables then we should have a linear combination of predetermined variables which would be independent of the error term and could be used in place of the y's on the right hand side. In the absence of a known reduced form, use of the estimated reduced form still provides consistent estimates. Let us now spell out this argument more formally.

The true reduced form equations for the $H-1$ explanatory endogenous variables $y_2, \ldots, y_H$ are

$$y_{it} = \sum_{k=1}^{K} \pi_{ik} z_{kt} + v_{it}, \qquad i=2,\ldots,H.$$

The observations on each of the explanatory endogenous variables are given by the matrix of predetermined variables multiplying the reduced form coefficient matrix in the usual way:

$$\mathbf{Y} = \mathbf{Z}\begin{bmatrix} \pi_{21} \cdots & \pi_{H1} \\ \pi_{22} \cdots & \pi_{H2} \\ \vdots & \\ \pi_{2K} \cdots & \pi_{HK} \end{bmatrix} + \begin{bmatrix} v_{21} & \cdots & v_{H1} \\ \vdots & & \vdots \\ v_{2T} & \cdots & v_{HT} \end{bmatrix}$$

$$= \mathbf{Z}\Pi_1' + \mathbf{V}$$

where the 1 subscript on the reduced form coefficient matrix indicates that the row of Π containing the coefficients of the first reduced form equation has been excluded—the reduced form equation for y_1 is not required. Substituting this expression in our original structural equation gives

$$\begin{aligned} \mathbf{y} &= -\mathbf{Y}\beta - \mathbf{Z}^*\gamma + \mathbf{u} \\ &= -(\mathbf{Z}\Pi_1' + \mathbf{V})\beta - \mathbf{Z}^*\gamma + \mathbf{u} \\ &= -(\mathbf{Z}\Pi_1')\beta - \mathbf{Z}^*\gamma + (\mathbf{u} - \mathbf{V}\beta), \end{aligned}$$

combining the two error terms. For practical purposes the difficulty with this expression is that the true reduced form equations for $y_2,...,y_H$ are not known. If Π_1 was known, this equation would give y_1 in terms of explanatory variables $\mathbf{Z}\Pi_1'$ and $\mathbf{Z}^*$ which are independent of the error term, and so least squares estimates of β and γ would be consistent. Although Π_1 is not known it is consistently estimated by ordinary least squares. The estimated reduced form will simply be a linear combination of the predetermined variables with estimated coefficients given by

$$\mathbf{P}_1' = (\mathbf{Z}'\mathbf{Z})^{-1}\mathbf{Z}'\mathbf{Y}$$

i.e. $$\mathbf{Y} = \mathbf{Z}\mathbf{P}_1' + \hat{\mathbf{V}} = \hat{\mathbf{Y}} + \hat{\mathbf{V}}$$

($\mathbf{P}_1'$ is a matrix with columns each comprising a vector of reduced form regression coefficients; e.g. its first column contains the estimated coefficients in the reduced form equation for y_2).
Using the estimated reduced form to replace the right hand side endogenous variables in our structural equation, we now have

$$\begin{aligned} \mathbf{y} &= -(\mathbf{Z}\mathbf{P}_1' + \hat{\mathbf{V}})\beta - \mathbf{Z}^*\gamma + \mathbf{u} \\ &= -\hat{\mathbf{Y}}\beta - \mathbf{Z}^*\gamma + (\mathbf{u} - \hat{\mathbf{V}}\beta) \\ &= -(\hat{\mathbf{Y}}\ \mathbf{Z}^*)\begin{bmatrix}\beta \\ \gamma\end{bmatrix} + \text{ error term.} \end{aligned}$$

The 2SLS estimates are now obtained by applying ordinary least squares to this equation, giving

$$\begin{bmatrix}\hat{\beta} \\ \hat{\gamma}\end{bmatrix} = -\begin{bmatrix}\hat{\mathbf{Y}}'\hat{\mathbf{Y}} & \hat{\mathbf{Y}}'\mathbf{Z}^* \\ \mathbf{Z}^{*\prime}\hat{\mathbf{Y}} & \mathbf{Z}^{*\prime}\mathbf{Z}^*\end{bmatrix}^{-1} \begin{bmatrix}\hat{\mathbf{Y}}'\mathbf{y} \\ \mathbf{Z}^{*\prime}\mathbf{y}\end{bmatrix}$$

The fact that $\mathbf{P}_1$ is a function of the error terms in the model (including u_1) implies that $\hat{\mathbf{Y}}$ is a random variable and we cannot evaluate the expectation of the 2SLS estimates by taking expected values of the two matrices separately. ($\hat{\mathbf{Y}}$ is a linear combination of predetermined variables, but the coefficients in the linear combinations are estimates which are functions of the sample disturbance terms.) However it is possible to show that the 2SLS estimates are consistent.

To summarise the two stage least squares procedure for estimating an overidentified structural equation normalised on the endogenous variable y_1; stage one comprises estimation of the reduced form equations for the right hand side endogenous variables by regressing each one in turn on all the predetermined variables $z_1,...,z_K$, and calculation of the regression estimates $\hat{y}_{2t}, \hat{y}_{3t},...,\hat{y}_{Ht}$, $t = 1,...,T$.

Stage two comprises a least squares regression of y_1 on $\hat{y}_2,...,\hat{y}_H$, $z_1,...,z_J$.

The whole exercise can be conducted at one go. In the above matrices we know that

$$\hat{\mathbf{Y}} = \mathbf{Z}\,\mathbf{P}_1' = \mathbf{Z}\,(\mathbf{Z}'\mathbf{Z})^{-1}\,\mathbf{Z}'\mathbf{Y}.$$

When we form moments such as $\hat{\mathbf{Y}}\,\hat{\mathbf{Y}}$ some of the **Z** matrices are going to start dropping out:

$$\hat{\mathbf{Y}}'\hat{\mathbf{Y}} = [\mathbf{Y}'\mathbf{Z}(\mathbf{Z}'\mathbf{Z})^{-1}\mathbf{Z}'][\mathbf{Z}(\mathbf{Z}'\mathbf{Z})^{-1}\mathbf{Z}'\mathbf{Y}] = \mathbf{Y}'\mathbf{Z}(\mathbf{Z}'\mathbf{Z})^{-1}\mathbf{Z}'\mathbf{Y}.$$

Also
$$\mathbf{Z}^{*\prime}\hat{\mathbf{Y}} = \mathbf{Z}^{*\prime}\mathbf{Z}(\mathbf{Z}'\mathbf{Z})^{-1}\,\mathbf{Z}'\mathbf{Y} = \mathbf{Z}^{*\prime}\mathbf{Y}.$$

This is checked out by writing the $T \times J$ matrix $\mathbf{Z}^*$ as

$$\mathbf{Z}^* = (\mathbf{Z}^*\mathbf{Z}\dagger)\begin{pmatrix}\mathbf{I}\\ \mathbf{O}\end{pmatrix} = \mathbf{Z}\begin{pmatrix}\mathbf{I}\\ \mathbf{O}\end{pmatrix}$$

where **I** is a $J \times J$ unit matrix and **O** is a $(K-J) \times J$ matrix with all elements zero. Then

$$\mathbf{Z}^{*\prime}\hat{\mathbf{Y}} = (\mathbf{I}\ \mathbf{O})\mathbf{Z}'\mathbf{Z}(\mathbf{Z}'\mathbf{Z})^{-1}\mathbf{Z}'\mathbf{Y} = (\mathbf{I}\ \mathbf{O})\,\mathbf{Z}'\mathbf{Y} = \mathbf{Z}^{*\prime}\mathbf{Y}.$$

Therefore we can combine the first and second stages to give an expression for the 2SLS estimators in terms of the original data

$$\begin{bmatrix}\hat{\beta}\\ \hat{\gamma}\end{bmatrix} = -\begin{bmatrix}\mathbf{Y}'\mathbf{Z}(\mathbf{Z}'\mathbf{Z})^{-1}\,\mathbf{Z}'\mathbf{Y} & \mathbf{Y}'\mathbf{Z}^*\\ \mathbf{Z}^{*\prime}\mathbf{Y} & \mathbf{Z}^{*\prime}\mathbf{Z}^*\end{bmatrix}^{-1}\begin{bmatrix}\mathbf{Y}'\mathbf{Z}(\mathbf{Z}'\mathbf{Z})^{-1}\,\mathbf{Z}'\mathbf{y}\\ \mathbf{Z}^{*\prime}\mathbf{y}\end{bmatrix}$$

We said earlier that 2SLS provides a solution to the problem presented to the instrumental variables method by an over-identified equation–the problem of too many possible instrumental variables. Now it is clear that 2SLS is an IV estimator using $\hat{\mathbf{Y}}$ as instruments. Taking the expression for the IV estimator on p.106, replacing $\mathbf{Z}\dagger$ by $\hat{\mathbf{Y}}$, and substituting $\hat{\mathbf{Y}} = \mathbf{Z}(\mathbf{Z}'\mathbf{Z})^{-1}\mathbf{Z}'\mathbf{Y}$ and $\hat{\mathbf{Y}}'\mathbf{Z}^* = \mathbf{Y}'\mathbf{Z}^*$ gives the 2SLS estimator as presented in the previous paragraph. The problem of selecting appropriate instruments has therefore been solved not by throwing some variables away but by taking $H-1$ linear combinations of all K predetermined variables. The linear combinations to be used have been obtained by ordinary least squares estimation of the reduced form, and it is possible to show that this is the 'best' way to select instruments. If 2SLS is applied to a just-identified equation, then the resulting estimates are the same as those given by instrumental variables and indirect least squares.

In practice, when estimating a single structural equation by 2SLS, one needs only to know what variables to use in those reduced form equations–one does not need to specify the whole model. All one has to know is what are the other predetermined variables in the system so that one can approach the first stage by writing out the reduced form equations for $y_2,\ldots,y_H$ – without necessarily knowing about other endogenous variables in the model or the form of the other $G-1$ equations (cf. discussion of identifiability on p. 61).

As noted above the resulting estimators are consistent but, as usual in structural equation estimation, one cannot prove unbiasedness. Again, consistency fails if any predetermined variables are lagged endogenous and the error term is autocorrelated. We can compute an approximate covariance matrix of the coefficient estimates in order to calculate standard errors and carry out tests of hypotheses, and we can calculate an estimate of the error variance. The estimated error variance is calculated exactly as in the multiple regression case (p.83 above) by dividing the residual sum of squares by the degrees of freedom:

$$\hat{\sigma}_u^2 = \frac{\Sigma \hat{u}_{1t}^2}{T-(H-1+J)}$$

Note that the residuals $\hat{u}_{1t}, t=1,\ldots,T,$ are given by substituting the 2SLS estimates into the original structural equation, as follows:

$$\hat{u}_{1t} = y_{1t} + \hat{\beta}_2 y_{2t} + \ldots + \hat{\beta}_H y_{Ht} + \hat{\gamma}_1 z_{1t} + \ldots + \hat{\gamma}_J z_{Jt}.$$

They are not the same as the residuals in the second stage least squares regression, as those have $\hat{y}_{it}$ substituted for y_{it}, $i=2,\ldots,H$.

The covariance matrix is estimated as

$$\hat{\sigma}_u^2 \begin{bmatrix} \mathbf{Y'Z\,(Z'Z)^{-1}\,Z'Y} & \mathbf{Y'Z^*} \\ \mathbf{Z^{*\prime}Y} & \mathbf{Z^{*\prime}Z^*} \end{bmatrix}^{-1}$$

and standard errors of the coefficients are obtained by taking square roots of diagonal elements, as before. Earlier, we used R^2 to measure the proportion of the original variance in the dependent variable explained by the regression as a whole. Now, however, we have more than one (jointly) dependent variable in our equation (despite 2SLS appearing as if y_1 were *the* dependent variable) so the meaning becomes none too clear. Further,

$$1 - \frac{\Sigma \hat{u}_{1t}^2}{\Sigma(y_{1t}-\bar{y}_1)}$$

can be negative, which is somewhat disconcerting. In the next section, we consider various predictive tests for assessing the performance of estimated structural equations.

5.10 *Criteria of evaluation, forecasting tests*

To assess an estimated model overall one needs a measure of the performance of the system as a whole as well as conventional statistics on single behavioural equations. In practice this means conducting various forecasting tests–it is often said that the crucial test of a model is an examination of its predictive performance outside the sample period.

The estimated structural form $\hat{\mathbf{B}}\mathbf{y}_t + \hat{\Gamma}\mathbf{z}_t = \hat{\mathbf{u}}_t$ gives us estimates of the reaction coefficients, elasticities, propensities, and so on. It can be solved to give the reduced form, and these reduced form equations may be used for forecasting purposes provided one makes some assumption about the error term. The simplest is to forecast it at its expected value of zero. The forecasting equation is then of the form

$$\mathbf{y}_t = \hat{\Pi}\mathbf{z}_t$$

where $\hat{\Pi}$ is obtained from the estimated structure as $\hat{\Pi} = -\hat{\mathbf{B}}^{-1}\hat{\Gamma}$. Notice that solving for the reduced form coefficient estimates is different from the first stage of two stage least squares, where one regresses every endogenous variable on every predetermined variable (i.e. estimating reduced form equations with no restrictions on the predetermined variables appearing in each equation). Most systems are overidentified and there are a large number of zeros in the $\hat{\mathbf{B}}$ and $\hat{\Gamma}$ matrices as a result of the theoretical specification. These restrictions are incorporated in the reduced form equations deduced from the structure. The forecasting equations will therefore obey the restrictions imposed upon the model, a property which does not hold for the reduced form equations obtained at the first stage of 2SLS. The argument for preferring the "solved out" forecasting equations is simply that they will forecast better if the a priori restrictions are correct. In practice, these restrictions may require testing.

We distinguish *ex-ante* and *ex-post* predictions. The former conform to the usual forecasting or future prediction exercise where it is also necessary to project predetermined variables during the forecasting period. Suppose we have a sample period $t = 1,...,T$ and a forecast period $t = T+1, T+2,...$ Then we must either use projections of the $\mathbf{z}_{T+j}$ variables, or use information about their likely future behaviour, and the ex-ante forecasts are given by

$$\hat{\mathbf{y}}_{T+j} = \hat{\Pi}\hat{\mathbf{z}}_{T+j} \qquad j = 1,2,...$$

How do we evaluate these forecasts with the benefit of hindsight? Assuming that the model is correct, that there are no specification errors, then in comparing forecasts $\hat{\mathbf{y}}_{T+j}$ with the actual values assumed to have been generated by

$$\mathbf{y}_{T+j} = \Pi\mathbf{z}_{T+j} + \mathbf{v}_{T+j}$$

we may distinguish three possible sources of error. The first arises from the disturbance term in the reduced form equation. This was set equal to zero for forecasting purposes, but the actual $\mathbf{v}_{T+j}$ will differ from its expected value. Secondly, our estimated parameter values ($\hat{\Pi}$) will differ from the true values (Π) – there will be sampling errors due to sample period disturbance terms. Thirdly, we may have *information errors*—errors in the predictions of the values of $\mathbf{z}_{T+j}$. These three contributions to ex-ante forecast error can be noted (in reverse order) by writing

$$\begin{aligned}\hat{\mathbf{y}}_{T+j} - \mathbf{y}_{T+j} &= \hat{\Pi}\hat{\mathbf{z}}_{T+j} - \Pi\mathbf{z}_{T+j} - \mathbf{v}_{T+j}\\ &= \hat{\Pi}(\hat{\mathbf{z}}_{T+j} - \mathbf{z}_{T+j}) + (\hat{\Pi}-\Pi)\mathbf{z}_{T+j} - \mathbf{v}_{T+j}\end{aligned}$$

Information error can in principle be eliminated when the forecasting performance is examined by using the actual realised values for the $\mathbf{z}_{T+j}$. This is what happens in *ex-post* forecasting, where we use the estimated coefficients but the true $\mathbf{z}_{T+j}$:

$$\tilde{\mathbf{y}}_{T+j} = \hat{\Pi}\mathbf{z}_{T+j}.$$

(Ex-post forecasting is really backcasting.) Ex-post forecasts can of course be obtained within a sample period ($\tilde{\mathbf{y}}_t = \hat{\Pi}\mathbf{z}_t$, t=1,...,T), which is implicit in the calculation of R^2 for a single regression equation, this being based on the differences between $\tilde{y}_t$ and y_t over the estimation period. The two sources of forecast error can be seen by writing

$$\tilde{\mathbf{y}}_{T+j} - \mathbf{y}_{T+j} = (\hat{\Pi}-\Pi)\mathbf{z}_{T+j} - \mathbf{v}_{T+j}$$

An impression of the likely size of these errors can be obtained from the results of the estimation procedure, for these provide estimates of the variances of the coefficient estimates (var($\hat{\Pi}$)) and the disturbance terms ($E(v_{it}^2) = \omega_i^2$). If a particular set of forecast errors appears to be substantially greater than would be expected on these grounds alone, then we conclude that the estimated model does not adequately represent the real world in the forecast period, and that the data no longer provide support for the original specification of the structure. (A formal statistical test is available for this purpose). Whether a particular structural change can be identified as the cause of the discrepancy, or whether a particular behavioural hypothesis can be blamed, is then a matter for detailed examination of the predictions of the separate varaiables.

Notice that there will be less information error when forecasting one period ahead if the forecasting equation contains a one period lagged dependent variable. Forecasts for the next period then embody the value of the lagged dependent variable in that period, but this is the current value of the dependent variable, assumed known. Let us make an explicit representation of a model which contains lagged endogenous variables by splitting the vector $\mathbf{z}_t$ into

$\mathbf{y}_{t-1}$ (considering only first-order lags for simplicity) and $\mathbf{x}_t$ (truly exogenous variables). The Γ matrix is then partitioned to conform:

$$\mathbf{B}\mathbf{y}_t + (\Gamma_1 \Gamma_2)\begin{bmatrix}\mathbf{y}_{t-1}\\ \mathbf{x}_t\end{bmatrix} = \mathbf{B}\mathbf{y}_t + \Gamma_1 \mathbf{y}_{t-1} + \Gamma_2 \mathbf{x}_t = \mathbf{u}_t .$$

Then $\Pi_1 = -\mathbf{B}^{-1}\Gamma_1$, $\Pi_2 = -\mathbf{B}^{-1}\Gamma_2$, and the reduced form is

$$\mathbf{y}_t = \Pi_1 \mathbf{y}_{t-1} + \Pi_2 \mathbf{x}_t + \mathbf{v}_t .$$

(Γ_1 and hence Π_1 may have a column of zeros corresponding to an endogenous variable which doesn't appear lagged at all.) For ex-ante forecasts one period ahead we use the known $\mathbf{y}_T$ values, project $\mathbf{x}_{T+1}$, and write

$$\hat{\mathbf{y}}_{T+1} = \hat{\Pi}_1 \mathbf{y}_T + \hat{\Pi}_2 \hat{\mathbf{x}}_{T+1} .$$

Thereafter, in forecasting $\mathbf{y}_{T+j}$, we use the forecast of $\mathbf{y}_{T+j-1}$ obtained in the preceding stage:

$$\hat{\mathbf{y}}_{T+j} = \hat{\Pi}_1 \hat{\mathbf{y}}_{T+j-1} + \hat{\Pi}_2 \hat{\mathbf{x}}_{T+j}, \qquad j \geqslant 2.$$

(This assumes that we are calculating a sequence of forecasts of increasing horizon as of period T)

Ex-post all the predetermined variables are known and we can treat the lagged dependent variables in one of two ways. We may either use the actual values or allow the model to generate a sequence of forecasts as a function of initial conditions, the forecasts generating their own lagged values as they go along, as follows:

$$\tilde{\mathbf{y}}_{T+j} = \hat{\Pi}_1 \tilde{\mathbf{y}}_{T+j-1} + \hat{\Pi}_2 \mathbf{x}_{T+j}, \qquad j \geqslant 2.$$

This enables one to study how the system reflects the dynamic behaviour of the economy over a number of periods.

Exercises

5.1 The following sums were obtained from 16 pairs of observations on Y and Z:

$$\Sigma Y^2 = 526 \qquad \Sigma Z^2 = 657 \qquad \Sigma ZY = 492$$
$$\Sigma Y = 64 \qquad \Sigma Z = 96$$

Estimate the regression of Y on Z, and test the hypothesis that the slope coefficient is 1.0.

5.2 If the 'true' model (in mean deviation form) is

$$y_t = \pi_1 z_{1t} + \pi_2 z_{2t} + v_t \qquad (t = 1,\ldots,T)$$

with exogenous z's, derive the bias in the estimate p_1 if the fitted regression equation is

$$\hat{y}_t = p_1 z_{1t} \qquad (t = 1,\ldots,T)$$

Under what conditions, if any, is this bias zero?

5.3 Suppose the true model is

$$y_t = \pi_1 z_{1t} + v_t,$$

but the fitted model is

$$\hat{y}_t = p_1 z_{1t} + p_2 z_{2t},$$

with z_1, z_2 exogenous. Is p_1 an unbiased estimate of π_1?

5.4 In the equation

$$y_t = \pi_1 z_t + \pi_2 t + v_t,$$

the coefficients π_1 and π_2 are estimated by least squares from T annual observations on y and z in mean deviation form; t is time measured in years about a zero mean (T is odd). Show that the estimate of π_1 is the same as the estimated coefficient in a simple regression of y on z^*, where z^* is the residual in a regression of z on time.

5.5 When error terms obey the following first-order autoregression:

$$v_t = \rho v_{t-1} + \epsilon_t, \qquad -1<\rho<1$$

where the ϵ's are serially uncorrelated, a regression equation with serially uncorrelated error terms may be obtained by replacing the variables y_t, z_{jt} with $y_t - \rho y_{t-1}$, $z_{jt} - \rho z_{j,t-1}$. (Check this). Suppose we apply this procedure to the equation

$$y_t = \beta y_{t-1} + v_t,$$

and rearrange to give an equation

$$y_t = \pi_1 y_{t-1} + \pi_2 y_{t-2} + \epsilon_t$$

where π_1 and π_2 are functions of β and ρ.
From estimates p_1 and p_2 is it possible to obtain estimates of β and ρ?

5.6 For the first-order autoregression

$$v_t = \rho v_{t-1} + \epsilon_t, \qquad -1<\rho<1$$

where ϵ_t has mean zero and variance 1,

(a) show that the inverse of the variance-covariance matrix $E\mathbf{v}\mathbf{v}'$ is

$$\begin{bmatrix} 1 & -\rho & 0 & \cdots & 0 & 0 \\ -\rho & 1+\rho^2 & -\rho & \cdots & 0 & 0 \\ 0 & -\rho & 1+\rho^2 & \cdots & 0 & 0 \\ \cdot & & & \cdot & \cdot & \cdot \\ \cdot & & & \cdot & \cdot & \cdot \\ \cdot & & & & 1+\rho^2 & -\rho \\ 0 & 0 & 0 & \cdots & -\rho & 1 \end{bmatrix}$$

(b) calculate the first order autocorrelation coefficient for the time series of first differences, Δv_t (i.e. the correlation between Δv_t and Δv_{t-1}).

5.7 In his capacity-output studies, Koyck estimated an equation of the following form:

$$y_t = \alpha x_t + \beta x_{t-1} + \beta\lambda x_{t-2} + \beta\lambda^2 x_{t-3} + \ldots \qquad (1)$$

(a) Transform this equation into an equation containing a finite number of x-values, and hence show how the three parameters may be estimated.
(b) What statistical problems arise in this estimation when a disturbance term, u_t, is added into equation (1)?
(c) Show that a final equation containing the same variables as that obtained in part (a) may be derived from a partial adjustment hypothesis, where the 'desired' level of y_t depends on x_t and x_{t-1}.
(d) When disturbance terms are added to this second formulation in what ways, if any, do the statistical consequences differ from those described in part (b)?

5.8 Consider the following demand and supply model:

demand function: $q = \alpha_0 + \alpha_1 p + u_1$

supply function: $q = \beta_0 + \beta_1 p + \beta_2 z + u_2$

endogenous variables: q,p; exogenous variable: z.

Do you expect a least squares regression of q on p to yield an estimate of α_1 which is too high or too low? Explain in detail. (You may assume that u_1 and u_2 are uncorrelated.) What alternative approach might usefully be employed to estimate the demand function in this simple model?

5.9 Consider the model

$$c_t = \alpha_0 + \alpha_1 y_t + u_t$$
$$i_t = \beta_0 + \beta_1 y_t + \beta_2 r_t + w_t$$
$$y_t = c_t + i_t.$$

endogenous variables: c_t, i_t, y_t; exogenous variable: r_t.

Suppose that observations on the variables are available for $t=1,...,T$.. Express the indirect least squares estimator and the instrumental variable estimator of the consumption equation in terms of these data. Show whether the two methods give the same answer and comment on the result.

5.10 For the model

$$y_{1t} = \beta_{12} y_{2t} + \gamma_{11} z_{1t} + u_{1t}$$
$$y_{2t} = \beta_{21} y_{1t} + \gamma_{22} z_{2t} + \gamma_{23} z_{3t} + u_{2t}$$

the sample moment matrices $\mathbf{Z}'\mathbf{Z}$ and $\mathbf{Z}'(\mathbf{y}_1, \mathbf{y}_2)$ are

$$\begin{bmatrix} 1 & 0 & 0 \\ 0 & 20 & 0 \\ 0 & 0 & 10 \end{bmatrix} \text{ and } \begin{bmatrix} 5 & 10 \\ 40 & 20 \\ 20 & 30 \end{bmatrix} \text{ respectively.}$$

Obtain estimates of the reduced form equations, (a) by ordinary least squares and (b) from estimates of the structural equations obtained using two stage least squares or indirect least squares. Why do the two estimates differ? Would you change your estimation procedure if it were specified that $\beta_{12} = 0$ and u_1, u_2 are independent?

REVIEW PROBLEMS

R1 Consider the following model

consumption function:	$c_t = \alpha_1 c_{t-1} + \alpha_2 y_t + u_t$
income definition:	$y_t = c_t + i_t + g_t$
investment function:	$i_t = \beta y_t + v_t$

endogenous variables: c_t, i_t, y_t; exogenous variables: g_t.

(a) Obtain the reduced form equation for y_t, and hence the final equation for y_t.
(b) Assuming that $u_t = v_t = 0$ for all t (i.e. the model is exact), and that $g_t = \bar{g}$ for all t, obtain the equilibrium value of income. Under what conditions on the parameters is this equilibrium stable?
(c) Suppose that, given time series of observations on y_t and g_t, we wish to estimate the coefficients of the final equation in order to use the equation to predict future values of income. What statistical problems might arise in estimating these coefficients?

R2 In parts (a) and (b) of Exercise 3.4, on the cobweb model, two alternative supply functions are specified. Given time series data on observed price and quantity, how would you determine whether quantity supplied depended on the previous year's price or on a forecast of the current year's price? State carefully any assumptions that you make.

R3 Consider the following model:

consumption function:	$c_t = \alpha y_t + u_t$
investment function:	$i_t = \beta_1 y_t + \beta_2 y_{t-1} + v_t$
income definition:	$y_t = c_t + i_t + g_t$.

endogenous variables: c_t, i_t, y_t; exogenous variables: g_t.

(a) Obtain the final equation for y_t. Under what conditions on the parameters is the system stable?
(b) (For the purpose of this part of the question, you may assume that the model is exact.) It is desired to stabilize y_t at a constant value y^* by choosing an appropriate constant value for g_t. What value of g is required? In order to carry out this exercise, is it necessary to change the endogenous/exogenous classification of the variables?

(c) Given data on the four variables in the model, how would you estimate the investment function? How is your answer changed if it is specified that $\beta_2 = -\beta_1$?

R4 (a) Assess the identifiability of the equations of the following models:

(1)
$$c_t = \alpha_1 y_t + \alpha_2 r_{t-1} + u_{1t}$$
$$i_t = \beta_1 y_t + \beta_2 r_{t-1} + u_{2t}$$
$$y_t = c_t + i_t$$

endogenous variables: y_t, c_t, i_t; exogenous variables: r_t.

(2)
$$m_t = \gamma_1 r_t + \gamma_2 m_{t-1} + v_{1t}$$
$$r_t = \delta_1 m_t + \delta_2 m_{t-1} + \delta_3 y_t + v_{2t}$$

endogenous variables: m_t, r_t; exogenous variables: y_t.

(b) Obtain the reduced form equation for y_t in model (1), and the reduced form equation for r_t in model (2).

(c) Assess the identifiability of a two-equation model comprising the reduced form equation for y_t in model (1) (an 'I–S curve') and the reduced form equation for r_t in model (2) (an 'L–M curve'). Given time series data on y, r, and m, how would you estimate this model? How is the estimation of the second equation of this model changed if it is assumed that the u's and v's are mutually uncorrelated?

R5 The following hypotheses are postulated to describe the market for a perishable product supplied by a monopolist.

(i) The desired demand for the product depends on its price and consumers' income, but in a single period actual demand is only partially adjusted to the desired level.

(ii) The price of the product is determined by its cost and the demand in the previous period.

(iii) The monopolist supplies whatever quantity is demanded at the price ruling.

(a) Set up a two-equation structural form to represent this market (obtaining a formulation which only involves observable variables, namely current and/or lagged values of quantity, price, cost and income).

(b) Discuss the problems, if any, which might be encountered if you attempted to estimate the model given the required time series data.

(c) How are these problems changed if cost becomes an endogenous variable, depending on current output? Outline the steps to be taken in any estimation procedure you propose to use.

OUTLINE SOLUTIONS TO EVEN-NUMBERED EXERCISES

2.2 $$p = \frac{\alpha_0 - \beta_0}{\beta_1 - \alpha_1} + \frac{\alpha_2}{\beta_1 - \alpha_1} y + \frac{u_1 - u_2}{\beta_1 - \alpha_1}$$

$$q = \frac{\alpha_0 \beta_1 - \alpha_1 \beta_0}{\beta_1 - \alpha_1} + \frac{\alpha_2 \beta_1}{\beta_1 - \alpha_1} y + \frac{\beta_1 u_1 - \alpha_1 u_2}{\beta_1 - \alpha_1}$$

3.2 $$y_t = \frac{\alpha + g_t}{1 - \beta - \gamma} - \frac{\gamma}{1 - \beta - \gamma} y_{t-1}$$

Stable values of β and γ are given by the shaded area:

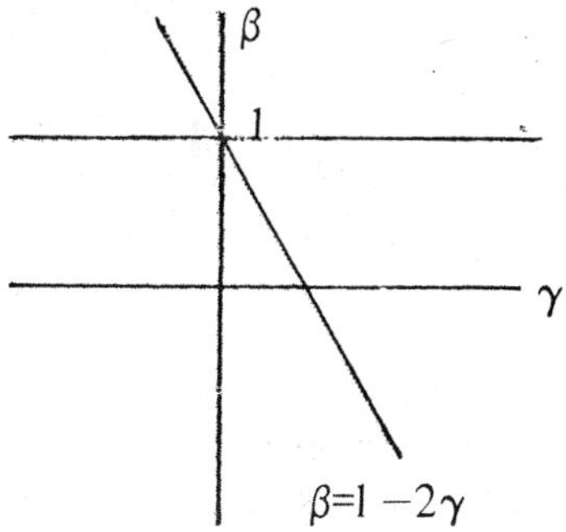

3.4 (a)
$$q_t^d = \alpha_0 + \alpha_1 p_t \qquad \text{(the "cobweb" model)}$$
$$q_t = \beta_0 + \beta_1 p_{t-1}$$
$$q_t = q_t^d$$

therefore $$p_t = \frac{\beta_0 - \alpha_0}{\alpha_1} + \frac{\beta_1}{\alpha_1} p_{t-1},$$

and the stability condition is $-1 < \frac{\beta_1}{\alpha_1} < 1$.

Thus in the usual situation with $\alpha_1 < 0$ and $\beta_1 > 0$ we require $\frac{1}{\beta_1} > \frac{-1}{\alpha_1}$, that is, in the conventional p–q diagram, S must be steeper than D.

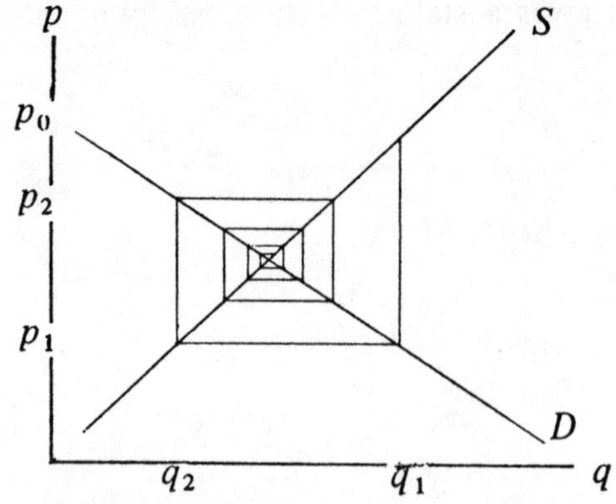

(b) The supply equation now is

$$q_t = \beta_0 + \beta_1 \hat{p}_t,$$

where $\hat{p}_t = \gamma \hat{p}_{t-1} + (1-\gamma)p_{t-1} = (1-\gamma)\sum_{j=0}^{\infty} \gamma^j p_{t-1-j}$

therefore $p_t = \dfrac{\beta_0 - \alpha_0}{\alpha_1} + \dfrac{\beta_1}{\alpha_1}(1-\gamma)\sum_0^{\infty} \gamma^j p_{t-1-j}$

By Koyck transform: $p_t - \gamma p_{t-1} = \dfrac{(1-\gamma)(\beta_0 - \alpha_0)}{\alpha_1} + \dfrac{\beta_1}{\alpha_1}(1-\gamma)p_{t-1}$

therefore $p_t = \dfrac{(1-\gamma)(\beta_0 - \alpha_0)}{\alpha_1} + \left[\dfrac{\beta_1}{\alpha_1}(1-\gamma) + \gamma\right] p_{t-1}.$

The stability condition is $-1 < \dfrac{\beta_1 + \gamma(\alpha_1 - \beta_1)}{\alpha_1} < 1.$

Assuming that $a_1 < 0$, $\beta_1 > 0$ as before, but $\left|\dfrac{\beta_1}{\alpha_1}\right| > 1$ so that the previous system is unstable, the stability condition becomes

$$-\alpha_1 - \beta_1 > \gamma(\alpha_1 - \beta_1) > \alpha_1 - \beta_1$$

so we have $0 < \dfrac{-(\alpha_1 + \beta_1)}{\alpha_1 - \beta_1} < \gamma < 1.$

Hence with γ in this range the system is stable despite $\left|\dfrac{\beta_1}{\alpha_1}\right| > 1$.

3.6 By repeated substitution

$$\begin{aligned} u_t &= \rho u_{t-1} + \epsilon_t \\ &= \epsilon_t + \rho(\rho u_{t-2} + \epsilon_{t-1}) \\ &= \dots \\ &= \sum_{j=0}^{n-1} \rho^j \epsilon_{t-j} + \rho^n u_{t-n}. \end{aligned}$$

As $n \to \infty$, this gives a stable solution independent of u_{t-n} if $|\rho| < 1$, namely

$$u_t = \sum_{j=0}^{\infty} \rho^j \epsilon_{t-j}.$$

Then $E(u_t) = 0$ for all t, and

$$\begin{aligned}
\text{var}\,(u_t) = E(u_t^2) &= E(\Sigma\, \rho^j \epsilon_{t-j})^2 \\
&= E(\Sigma\, \rho^{2j} \epsilon_{t-j}^2 + \sum_{k \neq j} \Sigma\, \rho^{j+k} \epsilon_{t-j}\epsilon_{t-k}) \\
&= \sigma^2\, \Sigma\, \rho^{2j} \quad \text{since } E(\epsilon_{t-j}\epsilon_{t-k}) = 0 \text{ for } j \neq k \\
&= \frac{\sigma^2}{1-\rho^2}, \quad \text{for all } t.
\end{aligned}$$

$$\begin{aligned}
E(u_t u_{t-1}) &= E[(\epsilon_t + \rho\epsilon_{t-1} + \rho^2 \epsilon_{t-2} + \ldots)(\epsilon_{t-1} + \rho\epsilon_{t-2} + \rho^2 \epsilon_{t-3} + \ldots)] \\
&= E\ [\epsilon_{t-1} + \rho(\epsilon_{t-1} + \rho\epsilon_{t-2} + \ldots)]\,(\epsilon_{t-1} + \rho\epsilon_{t-2} + \rho^2\epsilon_{t-3} + \ldots) \\
&= \rho E(\epsilon_{t-1} + \rho\epsilon_{t-2} + \ldots)^2 \\
&= \rho\ \text{var}(u).
\end{aligned}$$

The correlation between u_t and u_{t-1} is given by

$$\frac{E(u_t u_{t-1})}{\sqrt{E(u_t^2)E(u_{t-1}^2)}} = \frac{E(u_t u_{t-1})}{E(u_t^2)} = \rho$$

In general, the correlation between u_t and u_{t-l} is ρ^l by induction, for we have

$$E(u_t u_{t-l}) = E[(\rho u_{t-1} + \epsilon_t) u_{t-l}] = \rho E(u_{t-1} u_{t-l})$$

4.2 (a) (1) is not identified (rank condition fails), (2) is over-identified, (3) is not identified, (4) is over-identified, and (5) is an identity, fully specified a priori, so no question of its identifiability arises.

(b) According to the order condition, incorporating the homogeneous linear restriction, (1) is just identified, (2) and (4) are over identified, and (3) is not identified. However, the basic model is the same as in part (a), so we expect that (1) will again fail to satisfy the rank condition. Adding any multiple of (2) to (1) produces an equation satisfying the same restrictions, so (1) is not identified.

5.2 The calculated estimate is $p_1 = \dfrac{\Sigma z_{1t} y_t}{\Sigma z_{1t}^2}$

Substituting for y_t from the true model in order to evaluate $E(p_1)$ gives

$$p_1 = \frac{\Sigma z_{1t}(\pi_1 z_{1t}+\pi_2 z_{2t}+v_t)}{\Sigma z_{1t}^2} = \pi_1 + \pi_2 \frac{\Sigma z_{1t}z_{2t}}{\Sigma z_{1t}^2} + \frac{\Sigma z_{1t}v_t}{\Sigma z_{1t}^2}$$

therefore $$E(p_1) = \pi_1 + \pi_2 \frac{\Sigma z_{1t}z_{2t}}{\Sigma z_{1t}^2}.$$

So the bias is zero if $\pi_2 = 0$ (in which case the estimated model is correct), or if z_1 and z_2 are uncorrelated.

5.4 The multiple regression estimates are

$$\begin{bmatrix} p_1 \\ p_2 \end{bmatrix} = \begin{bmatrix} \Sigma z_t^2 & \Sigma t z_t \\ \Sigma t z_t & \Sigma t^2 \end{bmatrix}^{-1} \begin{bmatrix} \Sigma z_t y_t \\ \Sigma t y_t \end{bmatrix}$$

thus

$$p_1 = \frac{\Sigma t^2 . \Sigma z_t y_t - \Sigma t z_t . \Sigma t y_t}{\Sigma z_t^2 . \Sigma t^2 - (\Sigma t z_t)^2}.$$

In the simple regression $\hat{\pi}_1 = \dfrac{\Sigma z_t^* y_t}{\Sigma z_t^{*2}}$

where $z_t^* = z_t - bt$, and $b = \dfrac{\Sigma t z_t}{\Sigma z_t^2}$.

Substitution and tedious manipulation then gives $\hat{\pi}_1 = p_1$.

5.6 (a) The covariance matrix $E\mathbf{vv}'$ is given on p. 90., being based on the results of Exercise 3.6; the given inverse matrix is confirmed by showing that the product is the unit matrix.

(b) $v_t = \rho v_{t-1} + \epsilon_t$, with variance $\sigma_v^2 = \dfrac{1}{1-\rho^2}$.

$\Delta v_t = v_t - v_{t-1}$ has zero mean.

variance:
$$\begin{aligned} E(\Delta v_t)^2 &= E(v_t - v_{t-1})^2 \\ &= E(v_t^2) + E(v_{t-1}^2) - 2E(v_t v_{t-1}) \\ &= 2\,\sigma_v^2(1-\rho) \qquad \text{from Ex. 3.6 (b)} \end{aligned}$$

autocovariance:
$$\begin{aligned} E(\Delta v_t \Delta v_{t-1}) &= E\,(v_t - v_{t-1})(v_{t-1} - v_{t-2}) \\ &= E(v_t v_{t-1}) - E(v_t v_{t-2}) - E(v_{t-1}^2) + E(v_{t-1} v_{t-2}) \\ &= \sigma_v^2(\rho - \rho^2 - 1 + \rho) \qquad \text{from Ex. 3.6} \\ &= -\sigma_v^2(1-\rho)^2. \end{aligned}$$

therefore first order autocorrelation coefficient of Δv_t is $-\frac{1}{2}(1-\rho)$, which is always negative for $-1 < \rho < 1$.

5.8 Assuming that variables are measured in mean deviations, (and hence dropping α_0 and β_0),

$$\hat{\alpha}_1 = \frac{\Sigma pq}{\Sigma p^2} = \frac{\Sigma p(\alpha_1 p + u_1)}{\Sigma p^2} = \alpha_1 + \frac{\Sigma p u_1}{\Sigma p^2},$$

and we evaluate $E(\frac{1}{T}\Sigma p u_1)$ and $E(\frac{1}{T}\Sigma p^2)$ to obtain an expression for the asymptotic bias in α_1 The reduced form equation for p is

$$p = \frac{\beta_2}{\alpha_1 - \beta_1} z + \frac{u_2 - u_1}{\alpha_1 - \beta_1}$$

The required terms follow from this and the given assumption that z, u_1, and u_2 are independent, with variances σ_z^2, σ_1^2, and σ_2^2, say:

$$E(\tfrac{1}{T}\Sigma p u_1) = -\frac{1}{\alpha_1 - \beta_1}\sigma_1^2, \qquad E(\tfrac{1}{T}\Sigma p^2) = \frac{\beta_2^2\sigma_z^2 + \sigma_2^2 + \sigma_1^2}{(\alpha_1 - \beta_1)^2}$$

The asymptotic bias in $\hat{\alpha}_1$ is thus $\dfrac{(\beta_1 - \alpha_1)\sigma_1^2}{\beta_2^2\sigma_z^2 + \sigma_1^2 + \sigma_2^2}$,

which is positive assuming that $\alpha_1 < 0$, so we expect to find an estimate $\hat{\alpha}_1$ which is numerically smaller than α_1.

A consistent estimate is the IV estimate $a_1 = \dfrac{\Sigma zq}{\Sigma zp}$

5.10 The directly estimated reduced form is

$$\hat{y}_1 = 5z_1 + 2z_2 + 2z_3$$
$$\hat{y}_2 = 10z_1 + 1z_2 + 3z_3$$

The estimates obtained by solving the estimated structural equations, and which thus obey the over-identifying restriction, are

$$\hat{y}_1 = 5z_1 + \frac{10}{3}z_2 + \frac{10}{9}z_3$$

$$\hat{y}_2 = 10z_1 + \frac{11}{3}z_2 + \frac{11}{9}z_3$$

Under the additional specification the model becomes recursive, and the structural equations can be consistently estimated by ordinary least squares.

R2 The competing supply equations are

(a) $\quad q_t = \beta_0 + \beta_1 p_{t-1} + u_t$

(b) $$q_t = \beta_0 + \beta_1(1-\gamma)\sum_0^{\infty}\gamma^j p_{t-1-j} + u_t$$

i.e. (b′) $$q_t = \beta_0(1-\gamma) + \beta_1(1-\gamma)p_{t-1} + \gamma q_{t-1} + u_t - \gamma u_{t-1}$$

Following the discussion of section 5.8, we add error terms to both the demand and supply equations and assume them independent (both mutually and serially) whereupon the model is recursive with either (a) or (b) above, and OLS provides consistent estimates. The infinite distributed lag in (b) cannot be estimated, however, but a choice between (a) and (b) might be made simply by adding p_{t-2} (or a few lagged values) to (a), estimating by OLS, and if any lagged p's are significant, (b) is preferred to (a). The obvious alternative is to avoid the infinite distributed lag by transforming to (b′), but this introduces difficulties via the transformed error – note that *both* q_{t-1} and p_{t-1} are correlated with $(u_t - \gamma u_{t-1})$. However, if u_t is non-autocorrelated, q_{t-2} and p_{t-2} are appropriate instruments for IV estimation, and a test of the hypothesis that the model is (a) is based on the estimated coefficient of q_{t-1}, i.e. the null hypothesis is that $\gamma = 0$.

R4 (a) (1): neither behavioural equation is identified

(2): the first equation is identified provided that $\delta_3 \neq 0$, but the second equation is not identified.

(b) $$y_t = \frac{1}{1-\alpha_1-\beta_1}\left[(\alpha_2+\beta_2)r_{t-1} + u_{1t} + u_{2t}\right]$$

$$r_t = \frac{1}{1-\gamma_1\delta_1}\left[(\gamma_2\delta_1+\delta_2)m_{t-1} + \delta_3 y_t + \delta_1 v_{1t} + v_{2t}\right]$$

(c) Writing the two equation model

$$y_t = \pi_{11} r_{t-1} + w_{1t}$$

$$r_t = \pi_{21} m_{t-1} + \pi_{22} y_t + w_{2t},$$

there are two endogenous and two predetermined variables. Provided that the π's are non-zero, the first equation is over-identified and the second just-identified. The first equation is already in reduced form (it excludes r_t) and can be consistently estimated by OLS. The second equation can be consistently estimated by indirect least squares or IV (using r_{t-1} as an instrumental variable for y_t). If the u's and v's are independent, the system becomes recursive and the second equation can also be estimated by OLS.

LECTURES IN ECONOMICS 1

MACROECONOMICS AND MONETARY THEORY

Harry G. Johnson
London School of Economics

Professor Harry G. Johnson's lecture course on macroeconomics and monetary theory at the London School of Economics is internationally known as one of the most extensive and authoritative reviews of the subject. Its publication in book form originated in a move by his graduate students in the 1969-70 session to make a record of his lectures for their own use. Their notes have since been revised and edited by Professor Johnson and the result is a wide ranging but compact survey of the important problems, analytical techniques and results to be found in the literature, at a level of exposition students of the subject who have completed an introductory text.